Dear Pi

I see beautiful reading

BEYOND THE BOX

CREATIVE THINKING EXPANDED

for you on this journey
together. May this
bring you wonderment
and transformation!
Believing in You
Christi Corradi
Author Speaker Guide

CHRISTI CORRADI

Quantity sales special discounts are available on quantity purchases by corporations, associations, and others. For details, contact the publisher at the address above.

Orders by U.S. trade bookstores and wholesalers. Email info@BeyondPublishing.net

The author of this book does not dispense medical advice or prescribe the use of any technique as a form of treatment for physical, emotional, or medical problems without the advice of a physician, either directly or indirectly. The intent of the author is only to offer information of a general nature to help you in your quest for emotional and spiritual well-being. In the event you use any of the information in this book for yourself, the author and the publisher assume no responsibility for your actions.

The Beyond Publishing Speakers Bureau can bring authors to your live event. For more information or to book an event contact the Beyond Publishing Speakers Bureau speak@BeyondPublishing.net

The Author can be reached directly at BeyondPublishing.net

Manufactured and printed in the United States of America distributed globally by BeyondPublishing.net

BEYOND
PUBLISHING

New York | Los Angeles | London | Sydney

ISBN Hardcover: 978-1-952884-38-2

FORWARD

Christi Corradi has a unique voice. She is creative, full of life, and loves truly helping people.

I had the privilege of mentoring Christi in how to not just understand the Immutable Laws, but to live them from the inside out. She has then, through her unique voice, been able to touch and improve the lives of many, many people.

She first stepped into the deep dive work with me at a women's retreat. She described herself as exhausted and lost. But sparks of possibility and new life began to fly and by the time she got off the plane flying home, she had the inspiration and steps to put together a workbook that would serve many in discovering and creating the life of their dreams: "The Creative Way in 5 Minutes a Day."

Christi continued in the Life Mastery Institute (now Brave Thinking Institute) to become a Certified Life Mastery consultant and a recipient of the DreamBuilder Achievement Award.

For her to earn her way to that achievement, I was able to guide her from that place of being lost and feeling at the effect of her circumstances to teaching her how to operate from the Universal Laws. I watched her grow and not only become a highly effective and successful coach and teacher, but also lead her life from these principles, in her marriage, in raising her son (also a DreamBuilder) and in all her expressions of her creativity.

Now she has truly gone Beyond the Box having written a book that takes the concepts of self-empowerment and helps people understand them in a unique and different way.

Beyond the Box is meant to reach our entire world. It will change your world for the better for sure!

Mary Morrissey
Founder Brave Thinking Institute

ACKNOWLEDGEMENTS

I never thought it would take a village to publish a book, let alone a world pandemic. But that is what it took. Of course, when all the Covid-19 stuff started up, I decided to step back from promoting my business and write the book I had been dreaming of. And that's what I did.

My first acknowledgement goes to my husband who not only supports me no matter what, but also brings the voice of reason into what I do. Like my Viewing Point tool in this book, I feel that when I ask him for his opinion, he gives it to me freely, and I get to take what I feel is right. Together we make a great team. The pandemic brought our 22-year-old son home to us, and he also has supported me through healthy cooking, running errands, and computer help.

Michael Butler of Beyond Publishing (referred to me by Jill Lublin, a trusted friend), helped with every step of the publishing process and with so much of the understanding that was needed as well.

And the person to whom I am in deepest gratitude is my editing partner, Colleen Malone-Engel, who spent so many days with me on Zoom as well as without me, going through it line by line, going through so many iterations, and with such clarity perfected the content.

There were three of my creatives that helped me with image and concept: Julia Stege, who designed the beautiful cover and helped me have the courage to show up as my bright beautiful self; my brother, Tim Ammons, with additional graphics; and Stefanie Thueson, with help on the Tools and graphics.

My behind-the-scenes person is my assistant, Naava Dewey, who kept the rest of my business going, plus stepped in to work on the book project whenever needed. See, it *did* take a village!

And then there are the mentors who have taught me and held me:

The late Dr. Peggy Bassett, who loved me 'just the way I was, and just the way I was not' (she is the first one I heard say that affirmation).

Deep thanks to Dr. Michael Beckwith, who not only taught me so much about Spiritual Principle, but supported me in so many of my endeavors, such as teen camps and the belief in our son coming to us.

Profound gratitude to my mentor who never let me get away with playing small, Mary Morrissey. I studied with her closely until her voice was in my head. I learned to think in a way I had never thought before and to understand and rely on Spiritual Principle. And when I doubt myself, I know that she always believes in me.

Thanks to my friend Marilyn Schlitz, who saw me sitting in the airport and came over and said, "You look like someone I want to know." She later told me I needed to write my book, continues to support me, and believes I have a masterpiece to share with the world.

TABLE OF CONTENTS

MY FLYING LEAP
~ A TRUE STORY

I actually had come through an amazing healing journey already with my physical body, where through my work with my mentor and coach, Mary Morrissey, I went from being a victim of my physical condition to being completely well, traveling to France and painting sunflowers in the south of France. That was my image and my mental equivalent of healing, the visualization of seeing myself painting sunflowers in France.

Continuing this journey, I went into a deeper exploration of this transformational work with Mary Morrissey and Life Solutions. At this particular training, I got this deep sense of really getting into the game this time, playing full out. I was absolutely going to move forward. That was a code for giving up struggle and being a victim. Matt Boggs, one of the facilitators, was leading one of the workshops about being a speaker to build your business. I announced in that workshop, "I'm not a speaker. I'm just a coach. I'm not going to do speaking. I am going to build my business on the Internet!" He raised his eyebrows at me like, "Really?" I had this sense he had a feeling that I was more than that, more than what I was saying. I realized that I had a rattle going on inside of me. I took in his raised eyebrows, and I knew I had to really take a look at this. I was having an internal struggle. I ended up sitting at the breakfast table with him the next day. He told a really empowering story. I felt like he was telling me that I really needed to start looking at who I truly was and what I had to bring to the world.

On the last day of the training, we were doing a ceremony where we were walking into the presidential suite at the hotel, and it had these large, scenic windows. We were to go down into this room in silence and gaze out the window. Then, Mary was going to lead a process. I was towards the back of the line. It was quiet and sacred, and as I entered, almost everyone was facing the window, and their backs were the only thing I could see. There were a few steps to go down, and some of the trainers were giving us a hand to help us down the steps and guide us into the room. Matt reached out his hand to help me. I caught his eyes, and something inside me said, "I told a lie. That is not the truth about me. I am a speaker." And as I did that, I missed the first step, and I went flying into the room. I launched like an airplane, and I was in midair. The first words in my head were "Oh, sh*t." Midair, all in this second, I thought back about my hurt body from the past, and I thought, "Oh, no, not that again." I shifted my thinking, while still in midair, to "No— I. Am. Well." And I know in that instant, there was a molecular change, and everything shifted. I. Am. Well.

I came down, and I went splat! Right in the middle of the room, and of course there were gasps and everybody turned. There were two medical professionals in the room, and both of them said, "Call 911. This has got to be pretty bad." There I was on the floor, arms and legs splayed out. As I began to move, I started to feel pain, but stopped it with "I. AM. WELL." With this thought, I started to sit up. And I was absolutely well. In that moment of being midair like that, I know everything changed, that if I had not moved my thought to that place, I would have had a broken body. One of the trainers, also a medical professional, said she thought I had smashed my face when it hit the floor. Another doctor on the other side thought I had broken legs and limbs. And yet, I was well.

I sat up very slowly, and every time I started to feel a piece of pain in my body, I went right to that thought: "I. Am. Well." Mary came down the stairs, and she got down on her knees and she looked me in the face and said something to me. And I couldn't make sense of it. I've been at this place before with Mary where she has said something wise to me and I couldn't make sense of it. This time, I chose to listen. Again, an instantaneous change of my thinking. I said to myself, "No. I'm going to hear what she has to say to me." I said, "Mary, please say that again." And she said, "You told me you were going to get in the game!"

This was one of the most powerful moments in my life. I live from this vibrational place, the thinking, "I am well," and regardless of whatever is going on in or around me, I can move to that place of "I am well." This sense of wholeness is right behind my third eye, in my forehead. You might think it was the Divine speaking to me. But in order to "hear" it, it's actually a practice. Just like doing calisthenics, and it was all of the work that I had done up until that time, of really noticing what I am thinking, making deliberate choices of what I choose to think. It is practice that allowed me to actually change in that split second, to choose my thoughts, rather than them choosing me.

Wayne Dyer had a great way of expressing it. He said, "What do you get when you squeeze an orange? You get orange juice." Absolutely. The practice is to have so much of our being be orange juice that when we get squeezed, when we're in that hard, difficult place, what comes out of us is our choice of what we want to have come out of it. I had done enough practice and enough work connecting with the Divine and the truth of my nature, that when I got squeezed in that very difficult moment, instead of returning to my victim life, I went to my empowered life of knowing the truth of who I am and my connection with the Divine. I was squeezed, and what came out of me was: *I am well.*

INTRODUCTION

Beyond the Box goes even further than out-of-the-box thinking. Who created the box anyway? It is one of the very hidden and underlying paradigms from which we operate. There are perceived protocols of how to be, who to become, and what rules to live by.

In Beyond the Box, I will share with you a concept I call Creative Thinking Expanded. If you look up the definition of Creative Thinking, it means "to think thoughts you have never thought before." I have done this type of thinking since I was a child. While on long road trips with my family, I would look off into the distance to see if I could see things I had never noticed before, and put things together that were not the normal way of seeing. Oh, the stories that came to my mind! I was a great story teller.

Creative Thinking Expanded is combining new ways of thinking, thoughts you haven't thought before, and adding the Universal Laws, also called the Universal Principles. These are the immutable laws that exist and run us even when we don't know it. Just like the Laws of Physics they are invisible, gravity for example, yet we are always under the effect of them. It is the same with Universal Law. Many people have heard of the Law of Attraction, especially from the book and the movie *The Secret*. It says that what we pay attention to we create. There is only one Universal Law, but many different aspects of it, and we can learn from each aspect and apply them to our lives. The one Universal Law can be described as Oneness, Wholeness, or Love. When we learn and apply them to Creative Thinking, there is no box, there is no limitation, and we begin to create a life of expansion, joy, and fulfillment beyond our wildest dreams.

As you begin thinking thoughts you have never thought before as well as gaining greater understanding of the Universal Principles, you will feel freer to let go of status quo thinking and boldly design your life based on what your masterpiece is. This is what you were born to become and you will have a richer and more fulfilling life.

> **"It would be as if a king sent you to a village on a specific mission. If you went and performed a hundred other tasks, but neglected to accomplish the task for which you were sent, it would be as though you had done nothing."**
>
> **- Jalaluddin Rumi, *The Rumi Collection***

In this book I'm using my Mastering the Art of Life system: Design, Critique, and Create. The first four chapters will generally focus on Design: how to think beyond the box to create your life, and more importantly discover the masterpiece that is yours to give to the world. The next four chapters will focus on Critique: identify what is in the way and the tools needed to remedy that. The final four chapters will focus on how you Create that life of your deepest longing and live your life as a masterpiece.

The majority of people, especially in the western world, are on autopilot and most of those who aren't feel discontent with their lives. This longing inside them is the desire of finding what is their Masterpiece, what they have come here to give. I have a strong connection with what I call the Divine (please substitute your own term: God, Higher Power, Quantum Field, Buddha Consciousness, Universe, etc, so it doesn't keep you from hearing what I am saying). You will see throughout this book that one of the most important questions I continually ask myself is, "Is this what the Divine would want to be expressing through me?" Why would the Divine want to experience lack or limitation through me? The only time you and I are stuck is when we are not living in the full expression of the

Divine in our world.

This book is adapted from a workbook I designed entitled *The Creative Way in 5 Minutes a Day*. On a flight home from a seminar, I dreamed of creating an adult coloring book with purpose and depth that would include a vision-driven program, incorporating the elements and principles of Art in explaining the principles of life. The workbook is a tool that can accompany this book to enhance your experience.

I am giving you my best, and there is more to follow. However, this book will give you a running start at creating your life as a masterpiece.

I invite you to come to this book with an open mind.
Change the language when you need to, listen with new ears,
contemplate a new way of thinking in a way
you have never thought before,
but open to this amazing idea that
you can live your best life ever.

BEYOND THE BOX

CREATIVE THINKING EXPANDED

PART ONE

DESIGN:
WHAT WOULD YOU LOVE?

The first and most essential step of your journey of creating your life as a Masterpiece is to articulate a clear and inspiring sketch of your life, the design of what you would love, and that aligns with your core values. At first, this sketch will be a draft. As you continue this work and go deeper, more details will reveal themselves to you. You will learn how to use Creative Thinking Expanded to bring this best version of yourself from sketch to Masterpiece.

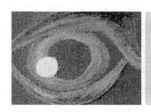

CHAPTER 1
WHAT'S THE POINT?

"The starting point of all achievement is desire."
- Napoleon Hill

What did you want to be "when you grew up"? As a child, what did you dream of, or play pretend about? And when did you stop dreaming?

Your dreams and desires are only one-dimensional, unless you bring them to fruition. And, quite frankly, most people don't. Using the art principles to understand the Universal Principles and how they apply to life, you start with "point." Point is one-dimensional. It is just exactly that, the dot on your paper, and nothing can become anything until you start connecting dots, creating the line. You become multidimensional when you move in a given direction, and most of us are living and moving forward by default. You have the opportunity to live by design and to start examining where you are right now: the point.

Living by Design vs. Recycled Thoughts

Those of you who have picked up this book, those of you who come to do this work, you are beginning to live by design, by choice. That's one of the secrets of life. The average person recycles most of their old habits and their thoughts to make their decisions and to move through life. These habits and thoughts all come not only from your past, but from past history, from the programming you were given. As a child, this was important. It kept you from harm, it provided the foundation you needed to grow, be safe, and become an adult. Humans don't fully develop the frontal lobe of their brain until mid to late twenties. This is the part of the brain that processes judgement and problem solving. This is actually when you begin to discern and reason for yourself. If you only try to change the conditions of a habit you want to break, and not the internal beliefs that formed that habit, you will not get lasting results. Before we were married, my husband and I hit what seemed like irreconcilable differences, and our first response was to go our separate ways. We realized that this same problem would just show up in our next relationships, so we decided to work on the problem before we split up. We have now been married over 30 years! If you want a different result in your life, begin your own creative thinking. You have the choice to instill a new way of thinking, rather than condition-based thinking.

Condition-Based Thinking vs. Creative Thinking

Condition-based thinking is letting the past and the outside world determine your decisions and how you move through your life, the ninety percent of those old habits and thoughts that run you. That's based on unconscious thoughts and habits.

Melinda was a client of mine. Her full story is included in *How Creativity Heals,* a chapter I wrote for a collaborative book called *Choices* by Cherri Gregori-Pedrioli. To summarize Melinda's story, she was a young mother with a seven-year-old. She very much wanting a second child, but was not succeeding in maintaining a pregnancy. One of the other challenges Melinda struggled with was that she had been the type of person who didn't trust herself, but rather, looked to authority around her. We worked on Melinda listening to her own intuition and practicing self-guidance. During this time, she became pregnant again. Hooray! But unfortunately, she began to see signs of another miscarriage. She went to the doctor. They confirmed the miscarriage and sent her home with medicine to help her clearly end the pregnancy. When she relayed the story to me a few days later, she said, "Christi, for the first time, I believed in myself, instead of the doctors." Though she recognized the signs of a miscarriage, something was different. She decided not to take the medicine, and went back to the doctor's office the next day. They did another ultrasound, and there was a second embryo. The doctor had not realized she was carrying twins, and had she taken the medicine, she would have lost this baby, too. She brought this pregnancy to full term and gave birth to a healthy baby boy. He became an integral part of our coaching group.

Creative thinking is discovering your own thoughts. Desire is a longing in you and a place to look for your own thinking. Your desire, your longing, is the masterpiece within you longing to come into reality. Not the desire out of lack and comparison, but the desire to become more.

This is also called inside-out thinking versus outside-in thinking. Outside-in thinking is condition-based thinking, letting the outside world dictate how you make your decisions, or what you expect in life, such as "When I get that job, then I'll be able to become more spiritual, because I'll have the time to put into it." Or, "When I get that book written, I'll become more successful." Inside-out thinking starts with what is within you, the knowledge and wisdom, to actually uncover all the things that are in the way and keeping you from living that life of freedom.

A Key to Your Success

One of the things that I want to help you understand in this work is that your fear, your stuck-ness, your limiting beliefs are actually the key to your success. It's the key to your freedom, and I'll be explaining more of that throughout the book. But the important piece of that is that you can celebrate it. When you are aware you're stuck, "Wow! Yay, I'm stuck, I am noticing that!" This is one of the most important new habits to learn, to notice when you are thinking thoughts that are not in alignment with the new design for your life.

So, just think of how that is changing your mindset when you make mistakes; feel your failures or your fears and start celebrating your awareness. You are on the path to freedom. (More in Part 2: Critique.)

What is Your Current Set-Point?

In this system, point is the place where you are now. You can look around you. You can take the average of all of your experiences, whether it's your checkbook, your relationships, your health, everything. It is your tangible evidence of your belief system right now, because your life and everything in it is a reflection of what you believe. The work in this book is not dwelling on your discontents, but using them for your further growth. It's knowing where you are, so you can go where you want to go. That is set-point. A dot is one-dimensional, but when you put the dots together in a chosen direction, they become multidimensional.

"Inspiration without action is merely entertainment."
- Mary Morrissey

Designing Your New Set-Point

Continuing with the art metaphor, a new set-point, start with the question: What would you love? This is the beginning of crafting your new set-point, a vision or the sketch of what you would love to create, your life as a masterpiece. The difference between wanting and loving something is important to understand. Wanting generally holds many of the limiting thoughts such as, what should I want? "I want to make money, so I'll take any job." But it isn't the money you're looking for, it's the freedom you want money to give you, and a job that's not right for you can be a stuck place in your life. Focusing on what you would love for your life is a resonance within your heart, and will lead you to a more fulfilling place.

**"Everyone has been made for some particular work,
and the desire for that work has been put in every heart."
- Rumi**

Asking yourself "what would I *LOVE*?" helps you bring that desire into your heart. It allows you to make refinements to the design, to look at proportions and balance (which will be addressed later in this book). You *can* venture out without a sketch, which is a really fun thing to do. But if you want to address that longing to accomplish something specific and bring your masterpiece into the world, it is best to have a sketch. It can and will change and morph, but if you want to create a life you love living, you will need to be the artist of your own life.

When we decided to remodel our kitchen, I found a contractor with good design skills. I had been clipping out pictures of dream kitchen ideas. I knew I didn't want anything "normal" or everyday, and I loved purple and wanted it to reflect that. If I had asked him to make me a beautiful kitchen, it would have been beautiful, but it wouldn't have been purple. If you let your life go wherever it leads you, it will probably be an okay life, or even a good life. But if you are still feeling incomplete or have a longing in you, that is the masterpiece you were born to become. You will always be restless until you bring that masterpiece into the world.

**"Your time is limited, so don't waste it
living someone else's life."
- Steve Jobs**

So, how do you begin crafting a new set-point? You start with where you are. Your current point. And you ask yourself, "What's not working? What do I want to be different?" Don't forget to ask yourself, "What were my childhood dreams?" You can also imagine yourself as an elder, sitting on a porch looking back over your life, the best version possible. What is that life you see yourself having lived?

Form a clear and well-defined mental picture of what you want. Do not specify a particular form of how it shall come, but simply desire firmly the greatest amount of good in that direction. Keep your mind gentle, avoiding a tense state of mind or any condition of straining or anxiety.

Many people get stuck at this point, because they're afraid they can't change their minds once it's written down. But a life design is fluid and changeable. What you're really creating is that vibrational frequency of what you would love. So dream away! And re-write it when clarity changes the picture of a new direction and possibly, an even higher purpose.

What would you love for your life, not worrying about how to make it happen? Don't just ask yourself what you would want. That limits you, because it is tied to what you believe you *should* want. Instead, ask yourself what you would *LOVE*. That allows you to dream and to do the deeper work to discover your life as a masterpiece.

Many people start thinking, "Well, I would like a million dollars," but truthfully, it isn't the money you want; it is the results. Believe me, it is easy to spend a million dollars and end up with nothing. If you think about the money as a means to reaching your goal, it will limit you. If you say, I want a hundred thousand dollars to remodel my kitchen, you may get the kitchen, but as mentioned earlier, it may not be purple (or whatever your color choice may be). Instead, expand your thinking: I love my new kitchen that fits within my hundred thousand dollar budget, and it has beautiful purple wooden cabinets and an island that allows people to gather around and cook together. My cabinetmaker gave me a quote on the purple wooden cabinets. It pushed me over my budget. Then, he said, "I know a store that has a stack of oak veneer that was a mis-order." They were selling it at a quarter of the price. It turned out that the wood-staining guy is part of a group of people I had gone camping with. He gave me a good price. It's not the money I wanted, it was a beautiful kitchen. Wanting the money is a "how." Ask for guidance to know what is yours to do. What is your masterpiece to bring into the world?

You are here to live in the flow, that greater expansion of the universal flow, the 'Ah!' over and over again, to be more creative, to love life more, and to experience bigger greatness and give your gifts, your masterpiece, into the world.

Working with my clients, I help them craft a three-year to five-year set-point or design of their life. It is best to have guidance to do this, as there is a science to it.

But if you would like to get started, here is what you do: Sit quietly for a few minutes and ask yourself, in three years from now "what would I love?" Don't worry about the how or the why right now, just let go and dream (the bigger the better!).

Think about how it will feel when this dream is reality. Use all of your senses to conjure up the true vision or sketch.

What do you see, hear, taste, smell, and feel?

Are you on a beach with sand between your toes? Or on a city rooftop looking at the night skyline of London? Maybe you're drinking tea in a garden that you created surrounded by a few good friends.

Write it as if it exists right now.

For professional help, you can schedule an appointment for a Sketch Your Life Session through Mastering the Art of Life.

https://maol.as.me/Sketch

❦ ❦ ❦

> ### *Law of Attraction (Visualization)*
> ### *~ Create a clear sketch of your life design.*
>
> Get a clear mental picture of your life design as you wish it to look when you get it. You must have that clear mental picture within your mind, never losing sight of it. It was the foundation for *The Secret*. This is important, but remember that Law of Vibration is the primary law, as Wallace Wattles teaches.

Tool: Using your Personal Guidance System (PGS)

Driving across the country is best done if you have a map or a GPS to get you to your destination. A Personal Guidance System is the same. You want to have a clear design of where you are going. Then, as you come upon decisions to make, use your PGS.

Exercise:

- Think of a decision or choice that is on your mind right now.
- Ask yourself, "Does this move me in the direction of my life design?"
- Why or why not?
- If it does, continue in that direction, even if it is a bit out of the way.
- If it takes you in a totally different direction, stop and get back on track.

CHAPTER 2
LINE, THE WALKING DOT

"A line is a dot that went for a walk."
- Paul Klee

Your New Set-Point

Now that you have a sketch (new set-point) for your life as a most magnificent painting, how do you get from here to there?

The journey to get there is to connect the dots. This forms the line in the direction of bringing your masterpiece into the world. You are beginning with a new, blank canvas. There are many paths, many methods, and you can end up anywhere without a sketch. That may be enjoyable, but as Rumi said, "It would be as though you had done nothing." Leaving life to its own direction, you may end up with a painting, but it is not very likely that you will end up with the masterpiece of your life. Now the line, the sketch on the new blank canvas can be dynamic; it doesn't need to be straight. But it *does* need to make sense. You can dream of a million dollars, but if your income is in the tens of thousands, or even hundred thousands, if you don't have something worthy of a million, you need to do the inside work. And it's not the million dollars you want anyway, it is the result of that money.

Now, the thing that happened when the book and the movie *The Secret* came out was that people started making vision boards. And then they waited for the magic to happen. Many of them missed a piece in there, because actually the Law of Attraction is a secondary law. The primary law is the Law of Vibration. You can't just make a vision board, look at it, and have your life match it. You have to *be* it, you have to *feel* it, you have to create a matching vibrational frequency of it. And that's what you're choosing: to move in the direction of what you are envisioning for your life. And unless you've done the work of creating the vibrational match to that vision board, things that make it happen cannot be attracted to you. People really got a little bit disillusioned when all of that happened. Many said, "Wait, you said if I made a vision board, I would get all of this stuff." Well, there's a lot underlying why they didn't get that stuff. One of the key problems is that they walked away and expected the vision board (something *outside* of them) to create the reality, rather than creating the vibrational match themselves. Then, that vibrational match *must* attract to you that design becoming your reality. See the Frequency Thermostat tool at the end of this chapter.

Steps in the Direction

Your daily work begins by asking yourself: "What is a step in the direction of that design that I can do today?" Even though you have sketched your three-to-five-year life design, you might be wondering how you're supposed to make steps in the direction of that dream now. You don't need to know the whole plan of how you will accomplish this. In this system, you begin with small steps now and each day. If you don't, you'll still be working on a blank canvas, trying to make a whole picture, a year, three years, five years from now. It is thinking there is a need to know every step before you begin that crushes so many dreams. The reality is, greater ideas of how to proceed will come from a greater source, which will be with you along the way, opening pathways you haven't seen yet, so just start moving forward.

My husband and I have done some dreaming together. And we have one version of a design of our future life that says we are going to buy a pensione on the Italian Riviera and have it both as a guest house and a retreat house for my programs. Why I said "one version" is that a lot of people also become afraid to make a commitment to a design. It doesn't matter, as long as you have a design that feels good and feels like it would move you in the direction of your greatest life. We could decide to move to Costa Rica instead of Italy; or even Santa Fe, New Mexico! All of those are dreams of ours. We have established a vibrational frequency of the details that are important to us. My husband wants to putter. He wants to garden and to take care of the yard, the pensione, this and that, and kind of schmooze with the customers. I want to have a beautiful environment to do my work. The primary action is to create the feeling *as if it already exists*, the vibrational frequency that's important. The tool at the end of the chapter will help you with this.

The important part of this process is not where you will end up, but that you know how you want to feel when you get to wherever it is. Because the "it" can change.

Let me explain further what I mean when I say you need to ask what is a step you can take today in the direction of your life design. A component of my life design is to travel and design travel programs for adults, creating itineraries and leading groups to foreign countries for enrichment experiences. I had formed a non-profit organization and we used to run youth trips for cultural understanding (Youth Beyond Borders http://youthbeyondborders.org). My dream was to expand on that model and design group trips for adults, the first one going to Ireland in 2018. When I asked myself what is a step I can take to realize this dream, of course I didn't just jump on a plane and shout off the gangway, "Whoever wants to come, let's go!" I took the steps to bring it into being. I started working on my budget for the Ireland tour, promoting it, and followed the steps to make it happen. After a year of planning and developing, the trip was ready to go and twelve of us had an awesome time in Ireland in 2018.

This is very similar to moving in the direction of that retirement dream that my husband and I have. And at this point it doesn't matter where we eventually retire. We may end up in Ireland. Who knows? We don't need to know yet. But dreaming about it is moving us in a direction of the feeling tone of the life sketch we have dreamed of. Now if you don't input something in your personal PGS, Personal Guidance System, you don't know which way to go, right? So, this helps us move in the direction. (See the PGS tool in Chapter 1.)

It's too soon to start packing boxes to move to wherever we decide to go. But it could be that I need to organize my desk, which would help clear my mind. One of the common complaints I hear from my clients is they don't feel organized, which could be the metaphor for whatever is in your life that's in the way of making changes. If you were an artist about to begin a new painting, you would need to clean your studio and put away everything you used on the last one you did in order to make room for what you need for the new one. Simply decluttering your environment may loosen things up for you to move in the direction of that dream. Or it could be having coffee with a friend who's from Italy or just got back to get inspired. It doesn't matter, as long as you take action in the direction. It notifies the Universe that you are serious, that this is the kind of person you are, and that you are moving in the direction of your life design.

There is another thing that you begin doing as you form your line. You begin critiquing what is in the way. Just as the cluttered art studio suggests, when you begin moving in the direction of your life design, things pop up and get in the way. Remember to notice what you are thinking and then choose thoughts and actions that lead you to where you want to go. This is when you need to become aware when your thoughts are contrary to your new set-point. Now, most people just say, "See, there are too many things in the way," but if you stop and notice, and even celebrate the noticing, you can then make a change.

Taking steps in the direction of your life design creates the vibration that pulls the desired results towards you.

"If one advances confidently in the direction of his dreams, and endeavors to live the life which he has imagined, he will meet with a success unexpected in common hours."
- Henry David Thoreau

Another Beyond the Box thought that you may have a hard time understanding is the idea *that you cannot get TO your lovely life; you must come FROM it.* And what does that mean? It means that at the frequency level in which you are today, you cannot turn your sketch into a masterpiece. How do I know that? Because it is still a dream. As soon as you vibrate at the frequency of the dream, as soon as you *become it*, everything moves in the direction of it becoming your reality. Advancing is about moving toward and confidently knowing and believing in it. These are the very key things. Sketch your life design, start in this work. You "will meet with a success unexpected in common hours."

Draw Your Line in the Direction You Want to Go

Imagine a line extending through each day into the future. You may always be busy with daily tasks, but hold onto that line, and know that every point on that line is taking you in the direction of your design. Even the smallest step along that line will be progress you can feel satisfied about each night.

There will always be chores to get done, but without a focus and determined direction, the years will disappear into mundane tasks without definition or form. Take time out from the tasks, the chores, to move confidently toward the beautiful, creative life you desire. That is what you came here to do.

I used this exact process to create *The Creative Way in 5 Minutes a Day* workbook, which is a companion to this book. Within three months' time, it was written, and I had it on the market. Below is an outline of the method I used:

- Sketch (write) your life design or project.

- Read it at least once every day for at least five minutes, <u>as if it's happening now</u>.

- From the belief that you are the person accomplishing this, what are three things you can do TODAY in the direction of the goal? (Remember, this isn't the how, this is the baby steps. We might call it the undercoat of the painting.)

- Prioritize those three things, and start at the top. Do as much as you can, and if you didn't get something done, reflect back on them and ask yourself, do I still need to do it?

- <u>If yes</u>: Roll over what you didn't get done that day. Yesterday's uncompleted steps are part of your three to-dos for the new day.

- Have a placeholder for those things you don't need to do yet, and schedule them later.

In the last chapter, you were looking at your current point and set-point, and creating a new set-point. I shared Paul Klee's quote in the beginning of this chapter, because I think it's fun and kind of cute, but also it illustrates what I'm presenting: if you have this old set-point, and design a new set-point, you have to start by taking one step in front of the other. You put the dots together to make them connect, to make a line, a path of how you will get from where you are now to where you want to go, your path in the direction.

Tool: Frequency Thermostat
(See Offerings – 4 Success Tools)

My Frequency Thermostat©

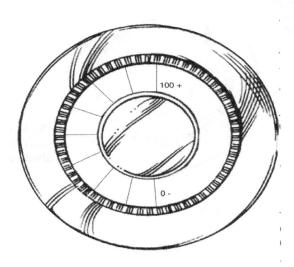

Using the image of a thermostat (above), turn your negative thinking up to a higher frequency! First, write down your negative thought, or a habit you want to change.

- Next, determine the frequency, rating it on a scale of 0 to 100 - with 100 being the most positive thought or attitude you've ever had, down to 0 being the most negative. You can give it a color, from 0 to whatever number your frequency currently is.

- Next, ask yourself, "At what frequency would I rather be?" Mark that higher number. Using a color that you respond to favorably, color the line from the number you've given the negative thought and up to the frequency number you would like to be. Focusing and thinking at that higher frequency, what comes to mind? What is a new thought or idea? Write that down for yourself, and refer to it as much as you need to.

My Frequency Thermostat

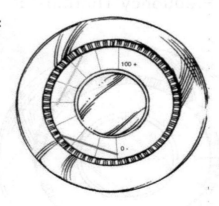

New Frequency:
The universe is
abundant and
so am I!

Old Frequency:
I can't seem to get
ahead financially

CHAPTER 3
SHAPE IT UP

"If you are building a foundation, you create a form to put the cement into. If there is no form there, it is just a mess when the cement truck shows up!"
- Mary Morrissey

Mary's analogy is about building a house. It is also about creating your masterpiece, and what a great way to say it. I say, if you're ready with your paintbrush and you don't have your sketch, your paint will dry.

I love the metaphor of the elements and principles of art for life principles. In art, shape is where you form a container by using line. In life, shape is the container into which you pour your life design. Let's think of it as a swimming pool:

- One side is, of course, your life design, sketch, or your new set-point.

- The second side is your assets: all the things you have done, all the qualities you are.

- The third side is your team of support. You are not in this world or in this dream of creating your life as a masterpiece alone. And your team members don't even need to know that they are on your team. This is, the people who support you. It would include supportive family members, teachers and mentors, friends, and even your heroes.

- And the fourth side is your passion and desire to bring this into the world.

Keep Moving in the Direction of your Dream

You can look around yourself right now and see your current set-point. Remember, if you want to know what you believe, look around you. Your life shows you what you believe. If you want to know what you believe regarding lack or limitation, take a look at your checkbook. It'll reflect your belief back at you. Whatever amount of lack and limitation you perceive yourself to have, your checkbook will reflect that. If you want to know how much you believe in or love yourself, look around you. Do you feel you are a victim in some circumstance? You may not see it, but events and people will show up to reflect that belief. And without awareness, you will blame them. But guess what? Your blame is misplaced. This is your thought about yourself. Not at the conscious level, but at the unconscious level. When you blame other people or events, you are a victim, and as a victim, you cannot change — yourself or your circumstances. When you begin to live these principles from the inside-out, you find your solid base and your strength. The good news is, you actually have the ability to repattern your internal beliefs. We will take a deeper dive into this in Chapter 7, Texture in part 2.

Emerson said: "Stand guard at the portal of your dreams." What *exactly* do you guard against? You guard against beliefs that no longer serve you, such as limiting stories of your past that you are continuing to tell yourself and reliving. Also, one of the worst things people do is they let the bad news on the TV and the collective status quo thinking influence their thoughts. Don't allow yourself to do that. It is about knowing and operating from the Divine Truth.

Eleanor Roosevelt said, "All the water in the world can't drown you, if you don't let it get in you." If you pour the junk in along with your new set-point, you will have to continue to do a lot of clean up. That's not all bad. Sometimes, when you see old thinking not matching up with your new direction, you can use that awareness to start cleaning it up.

Law of Thinking ~ Whatever you think
(or pay attention to), you create.

"There is a thinking stuff from which all things are made and which in its original state permeates, penetrates, and fills the interspaces of the Universe. A thought, in this substance, produces the thing that is imaged by the thought. You can form things in your thought and by impressing your thought upon the Formless Substance, can cause the thing you think about to be created." - Wallace Wattles

Tool: List Your Assets and Your Support Team
to Form Your Container

Write a list of your team, and be sure to include even the ones who don't know they are a part of your team. These are people who outright understand and support you. In your health vision, it will be your personal trainers and your other care providers. In your home life, it will be your family members and your best friend/confidant. In your career, your business partners and/or support team.

Assets: Having a list of assets is one of the most important parts of this work. It is a list of what you have accomplished and what you have become. This, of course, would be any schooling you have completed, any degrees you have earned, and any awards you have received. It also includes your roles in life: mother, helper, banker..." and then it is your values like family, kindness, leadership... and then anything else you have done in your life. In my program, I encourage people to work on coming up with a list of 100.

This is important when the thought, "Who am I to think I can accomplish such a large dream?" shows up. You have proof, and you want to pull this list out and say, "This is who I am, and more than this!"

And the last thing you pour into your container is the passion and desire to pull you through this endeavor.

Now, don't just pour everything you have into your container, you must be very aware of only pouring what you truly desire into your "shape!"

Container of Support

My Support Team

Mom, Sister Carol,
BFF Heather, Gym
trainer Javier,
Coworkers:Jake, Ben
and Tasha
Supervisor:Ruby
Aunt & Uncle Carson
Former Bosses Judy
& Hildy
Financial Planner:
Steve

My Personal Assets

BA in Psychology, License
in MFT, Bake killer pies,
Love animals, Volunteer
with Meals on Wheels,
Book Club President,
Public Speaker
Illustrator and Painter

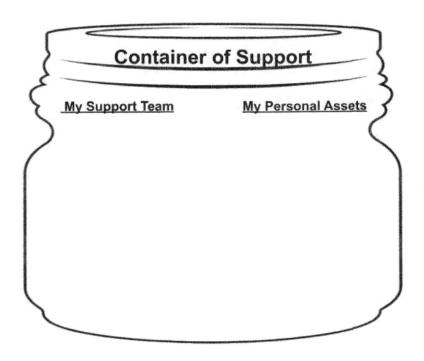

Container of Support

My Support Team   **My Personal Assets**

CHAPTER 4
COLOR YOUR WORLD

"I found I could say things with color and shapes that I couldn't say any other way...things I had no words for."
– Georgia O'Keeffe

Color. I love color. Color, in and of itself, brings me joy. And this chapter, Color Your World, is so potent. Color is the element of art that involves light. It is produced when light waves strike an object and are reflected into our eyes. In a sense, it is our perception. And perception is a choice, but as was mentioned in the intro, most of our thinking, and, therefore, our choices, are based on subconscious thoughts.

Of course, color is one of my favorite things. And in this metaphor, color is passion. Passion is any powerful or compelling emotion or feeling, as love or hate. You must have enough passion, not only to motivate you, but to push you through the hard parts.

Think of your favorite color or color combinations. When you see that color, how does it make you feel? Are there certain color combinations that excite you? Others that calm you? Others that repel you? There is a psychology of color, used especially in advertising. But here we are using it as the passion (or not) you have for your various endeavors. Let's take career. What are you doing and why are you doing it? Does it bring you joy? Or are you doing it just to make money, to make ends meet? Making money is not all bad. But, what does the money get you? Is it enough, and do you experience freedom of time? Ask if you are living life fully, living the masterpiece that is yours to give to the world, and if not, then ask why you are not.

How is Your Life Colored Now, and How Can You Change the Colors?

What does Color My World mean? This is from my *Creative Way in 5 Minutes a Day* workbook: "Color is light. As the light meets an object, certain wavelengths are absorbed, and others are reflected back to the viewer, resulting in the perceived color we see." This describes the science behind light and what actually happens in the rods and the cones in your eyes. It is such cool science, that our bodies work this way. And so, the result is that we perceive color. In a sense, nothing really is innately color; it is the *perception* of color.

The sister of a friend of mine came into town to visit her, and after the first day that she spent with her sister, my friend came back to me and said, "Oh my gosh, I just got right in there and I started curmudgeoning with her and kvetching." This was their historic way of being together, but my friend had changed and grown. And she said, "I'm going to really work on that tomorrow." So, the next day, she really made a conscious effort. Now, she didn't turn her sister's words around, she just stopped engaging in that type of conversation. Then, she looked for ways to change the subject then and there in a different direction. That's one way to Color Your World.

Changing Your Thinking Can Change the Outcome

If you want to know my best example of changing thinking to change an outcome, read the story of "My Flying Leap" at the beginning of this book.

"Knock on wood." Think about that. If you're knocking on wood, you're depending on something outside of yourself. Something outside of yourself to try to make yourself well. And yes, you depend on doctors and depend on your prayer practitioners and the like. But you make the choices to seek their help, you choose to take their advice or not, and you do the follow-up work. They are part of the means to the end result. But most importantly you have to remember they are tools for you to use as you see fit. I had two knee replacement surgeries over a period of 6 years, and I love my metal knees, and that I have my personal trainer and other outside sources, but I have to be committed inside myself in order to create lasting results.

Much of what Colors your World or what determines your actions has been created by generations of habitual thinking. A friend was telling me about the Callahan Curse that dictates her family. She said, "When a member of the Callahan family buys a new lamp, by the time they get home from the store, it'll be broken." I looked at her and said, "Gosh, you really want to own that one? You want to keep that?" "Oh, but it's a family thing. You know, it's the Callahan Curse." I said, "You know, you don't even use the Callahan name anymore, and you're still keeping the curse!" Her mother no longer carries that name either.

The facts are the facts, and these are things that you need to pay attention to. You need to pay your bills. You need to take care of a broken ankle. You need to take care of circumstances that happen around us, whether they are created by your status quo or some other habitual thinking.

This is where you can get the color from. You can look in your heart. And you can use that vibrational motion. I mean, think about it. Color has vibration. The colors you can see with your eyes have a frequency of 405-790 terahertz. When you create a vibration within yourself, within your heart, you are creating your own personal color of who you are. You've walked into a room, and over here are the curmudgeons, and over there are the bright, cheery people. You know, they're creating their own vibration. Being curmudgeonly is a choice (though it can be a hard habit to break), but it's not in anybody's nature. You can choose to associate with cheery people.

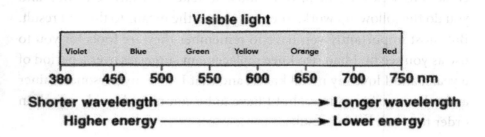

What are you going to pay attention to? A way I colored my life after my dad passed away was I crafted a very beautiful experience of honoring him, honoring my grief, honoring my feelings, and letting my feelings have a beautiful color. I think of it as a canvas.

Then, with the knee surgery, as soon as I could, I was inviting girlfriends over to paint with me. "Come, let's make art, let's be creative, I've got this window of time." I had people in my backyard paint with me. It was summertime; it was beautiful weather. Yeah, there was pain, and yeah, there was hard work and rehabilitating. Is that what I paid attention to? Only enough to get the things done. And then, I paid attention to the things that I wanted to create more of.

Adding Colors in Your World

So, what in your life have you colored in a way that you consider ugly and disgusting? What I would do with that thought is find other colors to put with it to make that beautiful. Ochre. I know some people call it baby poop color, right? Put that next to lavender, or a little stronger purple color, and it is a beautiful combination. Then, add coral to it.

Look at the combination; the ochre becomes pleasing in harmony with the other colors. So how does that relate to your life? For example, I hate doing certain parts of my job. I hate feeling like I have to convince people to come into my work. I know my work transforms lives. In order to reach people that want to make changes in their lives, I need to get my message out.

So, what do I do with that? I find ways of restating things. I love serving people and I am a heart-based person. That's what my marketing plan is. It lets people know how much I love serving them, how I create a safe and non-judgmental space for them. What I did for myself was one day I created a video of myself painting to share my message. Metaphorically, I can also use other colors, such as gifting my teaching calls on social media, and writing this book. That's the purple to the ochre. And if I have a painting retreat coming up, that's the coral. So how are you coloring your world, and how can you add or change colors to enhance the things that may not be working, as I enhanced my world that day I had to market on social media and chose to paint my message!

Law of Creativity ~ The Universe is always creating anew.

"Spirit thinks, and the world comes into being. Likewise, all human accomplishments originate in thought. Our human thinking process is a reflection of the Divine Creative Process in microcosm." - Ernest Holmes

Tool: Color Your World

Color is light. As the light meets an object, certain wavelengths are absorbed, and others are reflected back to the viewer, resulting in the perceived hue (color you see).

Think about it! All you need to do is change the objects (ways of thinking or past beliefs), and you can change the color of your life.

Another way to open your creative mind is to break free of expected thinking.

Everyone can hit rough times, and these rough times can "color" how you see so many other things.

1. Discover a discontent or a disappointment.

2. Now, think of your Life Design. In your mind, what color or colors would it be?

3. Using that color (which is a frequency), what is a step in the direction that changes your disappointment into something more in line with your design?

4. Be open to letting something unexpected help you color that disappointment.

SUMMARY OF DESIGN

Point, Line, Shape, and Color: all four of these things are important and are part of design. They keep you on track. They help you move forward, and they pull you up when you need it. Every day, read your vision in the frequency of it already being true (view your sketch or new set-point). Acknowledge that you are supported by the team around you. Imagine a pep talk from one of them when you need it, or reach out to them in person. Review your assets to stand on as a stepping stone, remembering who you have been to get the courage to move forward with confidence. Lastly, move daily to the feeling tone of the passion that drives you.

PART TWO

CRITIQUE:
WHAT'S IN THE WAY?

If you ever took an art class, you probably dreaded critique day. And in my experience, they could be brutal. Once I was out of school, I found some lovely critique groups that were helpful and kind. Reality checks are necessary, and you need them. If you truly want the benefits of this work, you will want to take a deep dive into the Critiquing process and get everything you can glean from it. It is an important part of the process if you want to go beyond the box.

Critiquing the thing that is keeping you from creating your masterpiece is about looking at what is in your way and how to change that. Everyone has unconscious limiting beliefs from the past, and yours are keeping you stuck today. These negative beliefs affect your emotions, motivation, confidence, and success - and they overall sabotage your results. But the deeper you go into practicing Creative Thinking Expanded, the more you will identify your roadblocks and limiting beliefs. Most importantly, you will learn how to create replacement thoughts that will take you Beyond the Box in your experience. The most surprising thing you will learn is that your blocks actually hold the key to your transformation. They are your teacher and friend. They will become the things that lift you up.

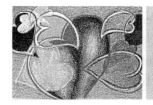

CHAPTER 5

VALUE: IT'S NOT ALL BLACK AND WHITE

"Things only have the value we give them."
- Moliere 1622-1673 French Actor and Playwright

Value. It's not just black and white. Just as color brings vibrancy to an image, value brings a picture to life. You know, when somebody says a picture is flat, you can generally assume that it is because it's only playing with the mid-tones of value, the lights and darks that are in the middle range, rather than including greater contrasts of light and dark. Just as the highs and lows of your experiences form your life, value shows all of the depth in your life.

The lightness and darkness are visually what give the appearance of shape. When you are clear on your values, the things that you want highlighted in your life, then the things you give attention to are the things that you draw to yourself. You can use value in the background to illuminate your life. Once again it comes down to: what are you thinking? To notice what you are thinking, you want to be constantly asking yourself, "What are my thoughts today, in this moment?"

What are the things that really are important to you? This is your value. If you think of the art element of value, you could call this your thinking source. What is it that you are shining on your life, your experiences? This will "shed light on" the thoughts you are thinking.

Discovering and Clarifying Your Core Values

The discovery and clarification of your core values is helpful to be sure your values are representative of you. As mentioned in Point, most people live by default thinking, recycling old habits and thoughts, and this includes the values you may have obtained from your parents or your past.

Having clarity of your own personal values increases your self-value and your self-worth and allows you to create your life in alignment with your dreams. Part of this work is about cutting away those that are not your core values.

Shed the Light on Your Core Values

As an example, my number one core value (actually two equally) are family and kindness. I believe they go together. When my son was in middle school, I was teaching high school art, working with at-risk youth. I would come home exhausted. Some of my students were out of juvenile detention, some of them were on probation, and some of them couldn't navigate the normal school system. I really loved working with them, but it was challenging, especially when I got some kids who really didn't want to be there. Or who felt they needed to uphold an image; you know that teenager "I'm too cool for school" kind of thing. It was hard work, and I came home one night, and my son asked, "Can I have some kids over?" I said, "Oh, honey, I'm so tired right now. I've been around kids all day." He said, "You give those kids more attention than you give me." And you know, he was right. I went to the school office the next day and told them I was quitting at the mid-term. I quit in the middle of the year. I made sure the school had somebody to come in behind me and things like that, but my son was my first priority.

One of the most influential things I learned in my training as a coach with Life Mastery Institute (now Brave Thinking Institute) is a list of five questions I am going to share with you. They were given to us, as my mentor Mary Morrissey would say, "to test whether your dream is worthy of you." And I love that, because you will be putting everything you have into your life as a masterpiece. Also, I have found that these five questions can be used across the board to see if you are making decisions that are right for you.

Five Questions to See Whether Your Life Design is Worthy of You

The first question: <u>Does it give you life?</u>

Are you just surviving? You aren't meant to just survive. You are an expression of the Divine, and in a sense, it is your responsibility to be that expression of the Divine in all aspects of your life. You may feel you have to work to survive, that you have to put up with unsatisfying relationships to be loved, and that you must fit in to survive. If you aren't feeling that you are living your best life, you may have the sense of self-judgement or overwhelm. Start right now, notice what you are thinking, and trust that this process will take you from one step to another to begin living the masterpiece of your life. Choose what gives you life.

The second question: <u>Does it align with your core values</u>?

Again, you must define your personal and true core values. What are your core values? Assess for yourself. Here are some examples:

<u>*Core Values List*</u>

Authenticity	Fame	Peace
Achievement	Friendships	Pleasure
Adventure	Fun	Poise
Authority	Growth	Popularity
Autonomy	Happiness	Recognition
Balance	Honesty	Religion
Beauty	Humor	Reputation
Boldness	Influence	Respect
Compassion	Inner	Responsibility
Challenge	Harmony	Security
Citizenship	Justice	Self-Respect
Community	Kindness	Service
Competency	Knowledge	Spirituality
Contribution	Leadership	Stability
Creativity	Learning	Success
Curiosity	Love	Status
Courage	Loyalty	Trustworthiness
Determination	Meaningful Work	Wealth
Fairness	Openness	Wisdom
Faith	Optimism	

With conscious awareness, weigh your new list of core values against everything: who you learned them from, how you interact with other people, what activities you are engaged in, even what TV shows you are watching. I had a client who couldn't get the negativity out of her head, and it carried through into how she navigated the day. In working together, I realized that she was watching gruesome and gory images while watching mystery shows. Once she changed the channel, those negative thoughts no longer dominated her thinking.

The third question: <u>Does it cause you to grow?</u>

If you are still living, you still have things to bring to your masterpiece. You live in a spiraling universe that is always expanding, and you are part of this universe. When you get too comfortable, you find that you are standing still, instead of going with that movement that is your inherent nature. You are meant to grow throughout your whole life. Even if you ask yourself, "Haven't I done enough?" What is often called life's third act is about growing into "being," gleaning from all of the past experience and accomplishments, and learning to be, rather than do. And that takes effort! So, whether you are in your first, second, or third act, you still want to be growing!

The fourth question: <u>Do you need a higher power?</u>

As mentioned, you live in a spiraling universe, which means you are always expanding. If you are doing something you already know how to do, it is not big enough for you. So, how can you expand on that? And I am not talking about something that is labor-intensive. In fact, one of the foremost reasons you need a higher power is to find ease and grace in what you do.

The fifth question: <u>Is there good in it for others?</u>

You might be asking how getting what you want out of life is going to be good for others. Perhaps you want to be in a committed relationship. Or maybe you want to make your living doing something creative, rather than what your family deems practical. But you being happy and fulfilled by your life's choice will make you a more productive person all around and uplift those around you. You were not put on this planet alone, and you are not a doormat either. One of my favorite quotes from Earnest Holmes is "for something and against nothing." Yes, even in my thinking towards politics. When you have a desire to have a love relationship, or a career direction that is not the most popular, listen: is that the desire of the Divine? Generally, it is, if it is good and brings no harm to others. And when you are in love, the other person in your relationship is probably feeling pretty good, too. But more so, think of the type of energy you are putting into the world: love exponentiated.

Building Confidence

As you define and begin to embed your own personal values in your conscious awareness, you build confidence. It is a practice. You can practice by creating statements around your core values and using it daily. Mine goes like this: "I am so happy and grateful now that I am the woman that values family first, serving others through my work, kindness, adventure, and living joyfully." You will of course make your own list as it fits your values and your life. Ponder the vibrational frequency of making this statement.

You can take a kind glance back at your past to see if maybe there are things there that are still holding you back. There is nothing in your past that holds you back. It's only your *thoughts* of the things from the past that hold you back. Think about it. None of your past is actually happening right now. It's long gone. But if you allow it to run your thoughts (usually subconsciously), it is a part of your makeup that makes you who you are. The good news is that you can change it.

How do you create lasting results?

I grew up in a relatively poor family. We lived for the beginning of the month, when the paychecks came in for my mom and dad. Big grocery shopping, and all the goodies: chips for our lunches, ice cream, Hamburger Helper, and other things like that. But by the end of the month, it was eating mayonnaise sandwiches. When I first started working, I could not save a nickel for the life of me, and I didn't know what was in the way. People would say, "Oh well, it's the way you're spending your money." Although that was the effect, it wasn't the cause. Lack of money is never the cause. It's your beliefs that dictate your actions, which then cause lack. In the beginning of this work, you've got to dive deeper and ask what is the self-belief that you need to transform? I had to transform the belief that I was poor and had to grab what I could while it was available. You can't make a lot of money and then change the belief; you will end up right where you were before.

Are you still that small child who was told they were weird? Are you still that small child who was left out? That's not true anymore, and even if you have those feelings, you are not that small child. There is the physical development of the frontal lobe in your brain, and that's when you begin to decide how to operate in the world, how to navigate, how to make decisions. But as a six-year-old, you just buy into others' beliefs, hook, line, and sinker. It is supposed to be for your well-being at that time, because you don't have the ability to discern the way of things for yourself. You are supposed to get all of that from trusted adults who teach you.

To create lasting change in my life, I had to practice the new thought, a thought of Truth: "I am a Divine child of God, and I deserve to have everything I love. That is my nature." I still have to repeat that. I still hit up against barriers all the time that bring out my boogeymen, that try to keep me from my goodness. Eventually in this work, you will begin to identify the discontented feeling and be able to move to a replacement thought of Truth.

Let me tell you about the Law of Sacrifice. I love this law, mostly because people cringe, and I can really get their attention. However, this Law is important. What it means is having passion enough for what you desire and identifying what things you need to let go of that are in your way. Perhaps it means letting go of listening to people who mean well by cautioning you against what they see as risks. Letting go of the habit of putting yourself down, especially when you are desiring success. It may mean cutting back on social plans in order to complete a project. Thinking of what you can let go of will help you throughout the four chapters in this Critique section, as you are on your way to creating your life as a masterpiece.

Unless you are very skilled at thinking only your own thoughts, it's not just your thinking; it's the influence of the thinking of the people around you. Sometimes, you have to consider what you need to sacrifice in your life. How are people around you influencing you, and are you buying into it? Additionally, you might have well-meaning people in your life who affect your self-value and your self-esteem by being overprotective, discouraging what looks like risk to them and hindering your ability to move forward in your life. Can you put up clear and healthy boundaries? Can you perhaps not fully let go of the beloved people in your life, but not let them activate the old habits, and maybe not interact with them in the same old way? Or in your own habits, are you spending money frivolously, are you wasting your time playing video games on your phone? The Law of Sacrifice is letting go of the lesser to experience the greater. What is your passion? Make room in your life to pursue it and be willing to let go of what is in your way.

What does this have to do with building your value and your self-confidence? All of the work that I'm presenting here is to help you build your belief in yourself, and therefore, your self-confidence. It's to help you use the sketch of the life you want to build, to separate your thinking from the pre-programmed thinking and practice living from your chosen values. Whatever energy created you and me, whether it's called God, the Divine, the Quantum Field, whatever you choose to call it, that energy is desiring to express itself through us. And why would the Divine want to feel pain, disappointment, struggle, or lack and limitation? You can return to your true nature, in harmony with the Divine. Even when the status quo thinking around you is saying, "You know, you've done _____ before. Look at what happened to you in the past." With new awareness, you can change and turn a kind glance to your past. You want to use the new awareness to highlight your values, to highlight the sketch for your life and the dream, through every action. Your nature is an expression of joy and abundance and gratitude. Hold onto that thought in everything that you do.

Law of Sacrifice ~ let go of the lesser
to experience the greater.

"Something always has to be sacrificed for something else."
- Raymond Holliwell, *Working with The Law*

Tool: Pause and Repattern
(See Offerings – 4 Success Tools)

As we've discussed in previous chapters, our thoughts are mostly recycled ideas and beliefs that we have gotten from past experiences and people in our lives.

The following exercise is about noticing what you are thinking and then repatterning your thoughts to work for you!

1. Set your phone alarm for random times during the day. When the alarm sounds, stop and notice your current thought.

2. Critique this thought.

   a. Is it leading you in the direction of your life design?

   a. Does it align with your core values?

3. Think of a thought that does lead you to your life design. Practice replacing the thought as often as possible.

If you would like that physical tool, I have developed an Excuse Me Button, complete with story and song. See the resources at the end of the book.

CHAPTER 6
FORM FITTING

"Only through art can we can emerge from ourselves
and know what another person sees."
- Marcel Proust

The element of form is form fitting. What is interesting about the term form fitting is that the truth is, as I said earlier in this book, if you want to know what your subconscious beliefs are, take a look around you, because the details of your life are exactly proportional to your belief system. What is so powerful about knowing that is you can change things when you start having your thoughts, instead of them having you. We are going to explore form and how it reveals the masterpiece within you, how it has been the way you are limiting yourself, and how you can expand your current container. Think of form. Form is the shape we discussed in Chapter 3, the container into which you can pour your dream. However, Shape was two-dimensional; in form, you are going multidimensional. How do you make it multidimensional?

Thought is What Activates Formless Ideas

The Science of Getting Rich by Wallace Wattles was written back at the turn of the twentieth century, and the language is a little dated. But the principles still fit the times we are in now. Turn off your normal-thinking brain, be willing to think thoughts that you have never thought before, use your current knowledge of the Universal Principles (Laws), and open up to more expansive thinking, in an even deeper way.

Wallace Wattles writes: "Thought is the only power which can produce the tangible from the formless substance." First, you have a formless substance. And thought is the only power that can activate this formless substance into the tangible. Again, Mr. Wattles continues, "The stuff from which all things are made is a substance which thinks." So that substance is thinking stuff, right? I'd like you to think of it as flubber, that jelly, googly, whatever stuff from the movie. When you think, you activate the flubber with your thinking. Through thinking or even observing it, or putting your vibration into it, it becomes a form that matches exactly that. As Wattles says, "The stuff from which all things are made is a substance which thinks, and a thought of form in this substance produces the form."

In other words:

- Your thought,

- Through your emotion (be it passion or disappointment),

- Causes you to move into action,

- And creates your results.

Now, to take it out of the esoteric, do you know what actually inspired Steve Jobs to create the Mac? He took a calligraphy class at Lewis and Clark up in Portland, and he loved the different way of writing. He was already interested in computers, and decided to find a way to make it possible to create calligraphic writing electronically. And this was actually the foundation of the Mac. First, he had the thought: how can I create something using this cool passion, putting this great groovy thing called calligraphy into use for people in the electronic realm? And remember: thought through you, into your passion, moves you into action. Steve Jobs took action, and that created the result. The window you look out of in your living room, the chair you're sitting on, the book you're reading, or the device on which you're reading it, all of these were first thoughts before they ever became form.

Then, Wallace Wattles goes on to say: "Thinking substance takes the form of its thought, and it moves according to the thought." So, it moves *according to* the *thought*. It doesn't move like you *wish it* would, or how you pine or long for it to. It works *according to the thought*. A great illustration, also from Wallace Wattles is this: "the thought of an oak tree does not cause the instant formation of the full-grown tree, but it does start in motion the forces which will produce the tree along established lines of growth." So, it's not going to come up as a stalk of corn. Because in its DNA it is an oak tree. But there is something called the Law of Gestation, which is so important in this understanding of this process. Inside you is a DNA; it is specific to *you*, just like the acorn. That doesn't mean that inside of you is *only* the DNA of a doctor, or *only* the DNA of a receptionist. It means that the DNA inside of you are the qualities that bring you joy, life, and freedom. *You* get to determine where you plant that acorn, and how you nurture it. I could have been an amazing accountant. I know I could. But the desire in me caused me to nurture making art, being creative, and to think thoughts I had never thought before. And this became Creative Thinking Expanded. That's how *you* get to take the DNA that's inside of you, and *you* get to determine where you plant it and how you nurture it.

Be Patient as You Wait to Manifest

Warren Buffett wrote an article on the Law of Gestation, and what he said is, "The amount of time required from the seed to whatever the seed becomes is the Law of Gestation. If there is any amount of time required for an acorn to become a mighty oak, there is an amount of time required for thoughts to become things." He said, "Honoring that there is an amount of time required is one of the best things. Most people start giving up on the idea or project before it comes to fruition. They pull up the roots, looking for the fruit, when the seed hadn't even been given time to grow into a fruit tree, let alone produce fruit." So, if you planted some seeds of ideas or projects, give them some time. Keep nurturing them. Water those ideas. Dig deep in the soil of becoming and let your ideas become results. Some things, no matter how great the talent or effort, just take time.

Watch Out for Limited Thinking

In order to critique what is in your way and create lasting results, in the beginning, you want to learn how to identify the block. With experience in this, eventually, you will be able to just notice that you have discontent, and ask yourself, how do I want to feel? And simply jump right to the new thought.

It is always your thinking, it is always your beliefs that are running you. You may say, but there was an earthquake, and it happened to me. Yes, on the factual level, it happened. But on the principle side of things, what do you do with that?

I want to tell you a little story (actually an adapted version of an old teaching story). My dad and I used to go fishing all the time, and it's one of my favorite fondest memories of my growing up, spending time with my dad fishing. One time, we were at the side of a lake, and you know you've got to claim your space, and you can't disrupt other people's space. There was another old fisherman down there, and he kept catching fish, and we hadn't caught any fish yet. My dad and I watched him and tried to figure out what bait he was putting on and his fishing techniques. Well, every time he'd catch a fish, he'd pull out this broken-off ruler and hold it up to the fish, and the ones that were bigger than the broken ruler, he would throw back in the lake. The ones that were smaller, he would keep. My dad and I wondered if it was because the smaller fish were tastier, or if there was some limitation we didn't know about fishing in this lake. What was it? Finally, since I was a little nosy and friendly kid, I wandered down there and I asked, "Hey, how's it going? What kind of bait are you using?" This is how you talk with the other fishermen; I'd learned that from my dad. He said whatever it was that he was using. I said, "You're sure catching a lot of fish. You're throwing the big ones back in. Are they just not as tasty? Not as good?" He said, "Oh, no." He pulls out his old broken-off ruler and he says, "This is the size of my frying pan at home." I just thought that was the most bizarre thing I ever heard, and I went back laughing and told my dad, "He was throwing in the big ones because they won't fit in his frying pan!" Now *there* is limited thinking, right? How much of your thinking are you throwing out because it doesn't fit into what your status quo thinking is? And what you have begun to believe?

Thoughts vs. Fact

Let me illustrate a concept and provide a language for you to be able to further understand Divine Principle or Universal Law. Let's imagine that the Law is represented by a vertical axis. (I will also refer to this as Divine, God, Principle, etc.) Remember, it doesn't matter what religion you are, or if you are not religious, or your political background or culture. This is true across the board for all matter on the earth. Just like the law of gravity, it responds the same all the time. In this illustration, The **Truth** runs on the vertical axis, and the **Facts** in this physical world are on the horizontal plane.

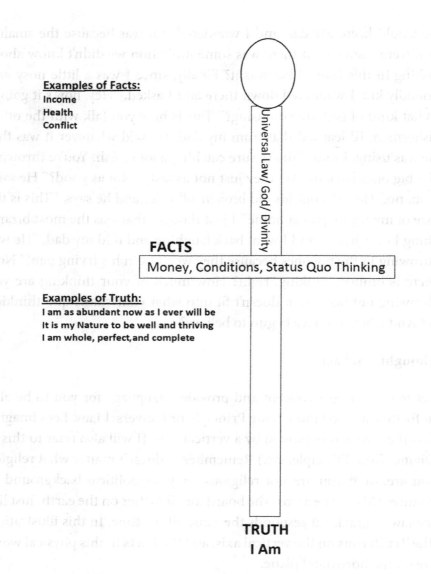

Examples of Facts:
Income
Health
Conflict

Universal Law/ God/ Divinity

FACTS
Money, Conditions, Status Quo Thinking

Examples of Truth:
I am as abundant now as I ever will be
It is my Nature to be well and thriving
I am whole, perfect, and complete

TRUTH
I Am

The horizontal axis is where money, health, all of the circumstances you have in life, anything that is changeable, resides. They all sit along that line like birds on a wire. One way to determine whether something is a **fact** (vs. truth), is that it is changeable. Your money situation changes, and your health may improve or not. The horizontal axis is your humanity, the facts, and the way things show up on this planet earth.

The vertical line represents **truth**, and it does not change. On this axis is where you find immutable laws of physics, of gravity, of math. But for this work, you are paying attention to the immutable Universal Principles. No matter what is going on around you, they are ALWAYS the same. Even during the pandemic. And when you learn to understand and use the Universal Principles, you are working with true nature, even yours. Your true nature is that you are Divine. Your nature is to be the full expression of the masterpiece within you. You are meant to thrive. You are meant to be happy. You are meant to give your gift/your masterpiece to the world. Anything contrary to that is not true and does not live on that vertical axis.

Discovering and Changing Erroneous Thoughts

The more you understand the principles that govern you, the Universe, everything, the more you can move, influence, and change your results on the **fact** axis. Again, as mentioned so many times, your current beliefs, especially the underlying beliefs, are reflected in your current results.

You're dragging your old stuff around, so you need to be aware of what you're thinking. Look at what instances you have discontent. See if you can identify the beliefs that might have you stuck. See if you can practice using a new thought of how you would like to think when you feel that discontent. I call these remedy thoughts. They will remind you that you are Divine, and that is your true nature.

Eventually, you won't have to dig up the old issue that created the discontent. You just need to know that there is something stopping you from being where you want to be. Then, you get to create the replacement thought, without even knowing what it's replacing. Your past is only alive when it's in your mind. And that is a great place to start understanding the replacement process.

Practice this: stand and look at your life as it is right now. Are you longing for greater abundance in your life? Then, replace your old thought with "I am abundant." If you are feeling low, replace it with "I am an expression of the Divine, full of vitality, energy, and joy!" And then, repeat. Repeat all the time, every day, every time you catch yourself believing something different.

You have the opportunity to create lasting change. It starts with your study and understanding of the Immutable Principles. In each chapter, there is a focus on a principle, and this will get you started. This next illustration shows you how it works:

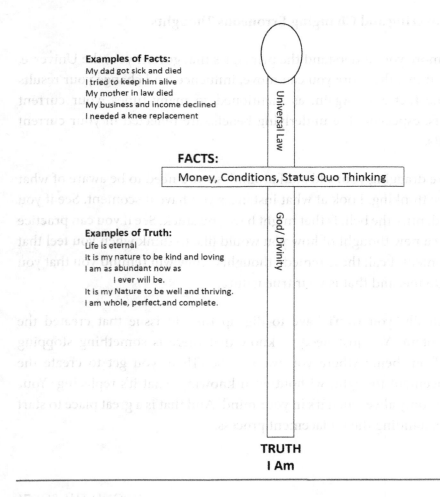

Examples of Facts:
My dad got sick and died
I tried to keep him alive
My mother in law died
My business and income declined
I needed a knee replacement

Universal Law

FACTS:
Money, Conditions, Status Quo Thinking

God/ Divinity

Examples of Truth:
Life is eternal
It is my nature to be kind and loving
I am as abundant now as
    I ever will be.
It is my Nature to be well and thriving.
I am whole, perfect, and complete.

TRUTH
I Am

As you see, I like to put an oval at the top of the diagram; it represents a person. You can use your body to remember this process.

I will use myself for this. Let's begin with a problem that is living on the factual axis: When I was taking care of my dad, my business and income declined. Notice the intersection of the two axes in the illustration. This represents your level of understanding of principle, and it determines your result on the factual level. As you practice working with the Law, you will find that your facts and your circumstances will change.

This is the truth of who I am: I am well, the Divine always has my back, I am creative. As I remember those truths, I begin responding to the facts from a higher understanding. What can I do with what I have, regardless of conditions around me? When the Pandemic hit in March 2020, I said, Oh…! I can do some personal deepening work. And, oh…! I have time to write the book I've had in mind! Think about the truth of who you are, and ask yourself what you can do with what you have, regardless of the conditions around you?

As I practice living from a greater truth, (diagram A) rather than the outside conditions, the more my facts will change. The Laws presented in this book are guides for you and me to stay in Truth. And eventually, the actual bar on which those facts rest will raise and begin producing results at that level. (Diagram B) Not just how I respond, but the actual results I manifest will be from this higher understanding. If my health is challenged, yes I take care of the facts, but as in my story at the beginning of the book, The Flying Leap, my results will be different. *I am well.*

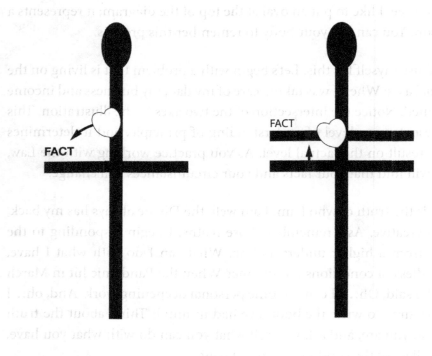

Diagram A   Diagram B

An Example of Using Facts vs. Truth

I call 2013 my year of surrender. In January, my dad got very sick. I did everything possible to keep my dad alive. I was at the hospital daily until he passed on January 14. Just three days before he died, my mother-in-law's board and care called my husband and said that they had called hospice. So, I spent that evening with my husband and his mother while she passed away.

I had one eye (a sleepy eye) on my business, which was just maintaining, and my other eye on my dad. My business really suffered. Then, in February, I had a knee replacement.

Let me explain how using fact versus truth works: My husband and I tried our best with our parents. And life is eternal. As a therapist, I know the stages of grief, and I was no exception. There was extreme sadness of course, but there also was a richness, a joyousness in tending them, and honoring them in their death. It was actually even more poignant when my mother was passing a few years later and was in our home for her journey to eternal life (whatever that is).

Although I barely kept my business afloat, I was blessed to be able to be available for my parents. I am abundant. And in focusing on my health, I was able to have time off of my work to recover, and I rolled that into a trip with my husband and son to Ireland. That led to taking the first of my travel groups there the following year. It is my nature to experience joy and creativity.

We live on the factual plane here, and I am not exempt from that. In fact, I don't want to be exempt from that, because this is the prize, to live here on this earth, "to suck out all the marrow of life," as Thoreau would say. And then, the second prize is to realize that we're able to live here in this life and create and design it in a way that brings us joy and freedom and goodness. And we do that by using Creative Thinking Expanded.

Form is the Result of All of the Elements Brought Together

Form is actually the life that you want to create. You have the opportunity now of looking at the point (where you are now), and your new set-point (where you want to go), and drawing a line that connects those two points. Then, joining the two ends of the line, you make the shape, like a circle, and thus create a container to pour your dream into. Going further with the multidimensional quality of form, you add color, which is the passion to move you into action. The value brings it to life and allows you to experience the feeling tone of the sketch of your life. So, through your thinking, you move toward your life design.

🌱 🌱 🌱

Law of Gestation

~ When you plant a seed, or your life design, you need to be patient, nurture, and let it grow. There is a time for every season.

"The universal Law of Gestation states that every process needs to go through a period of time during which it is conceptualized and actualized. Well, the same is true for our dreams and goals. They must develop on the inside, before they can manifest into reality. And that's why patience is required to achieve your goals. Have patience and believe in the end result!" - Bob Proctor

Tool: Feelings, Facts, Truth
(See Offerings – 4 Success Tools)

Your objective in this practice is to wean your mind away from self-defeating thoughts and nourish it, instead, with a consistently powerful exchange between the heart of your soul and the Universe.

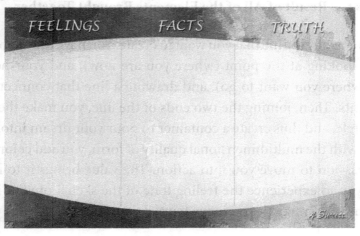

Use your Feelings, Facts, and Truth Board (above) to populate your mind with thoughts that are aligned with a higher truth, and your dreams, upgrading your standard "take" on things whenever your feelings signal a gap between what you could call "reality" and how you prefer to live. Here's how:

- What feeling has taken over, upsetting you and/or derailing your movement forward? Capture it in the first column.
- What could you take as the facts of the situation? Imagine their importance shrinking as you write in column two.
- Now, allow yourself to transcend appearances and consider the energy that has but one reason to exist: your good. Imagine that truth glowing with vitality as you write in column three.
- Turn your thoughts to the good unfolding now – just for you – and put your efforts into preparation!

Use your Feeling, Facts, Truth Board whenever appearances and your initial feelings cloud your knowing.

Write the truth – take back your power!

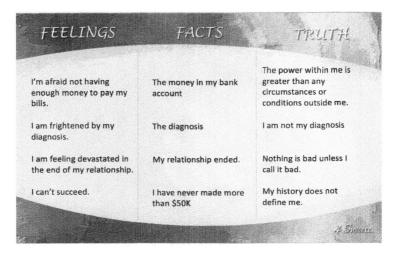

FEELINGS	FACTS	TRUTH
I'm afraid not having enough money to pay my bills.	The money in my bank account	The power within me is greater than any circumstances or conditions outside me.
I am frightened by my diagnosis.	The diagnosis	I am not my diagnosis
I am feeling devastated in the end of my relationship.	My relationship ended.	Nothing is bad unless I call it bad.
I can't succeed.	I have never made more than $50K	My history does not define me.

CHAPTER 7
TEXTURE OF LIFE

"There is something magical in seeing what you can do, what texture and tone and color you can produce."
- from *The Creative Way in 5 Minutes a Day* workbook

The wonder and the joy of texture is that you can create beautiful things, but often, you have to pay attention to your thinking in order to get what you want. In undergraduate school, I was in fiber arts, which included weaving. When I strung the loom with the warp thread, I had to be sure to be deliberate about making sure they were strong enough, and that they had the right undercolor for the desired results. The warp can represent your values, your beliefs, and your vision. But the shuttle, the weft, represents your actions (it's called throwing the shuttle), what it is that you are doing on a daily basis to create the texture of your life. When you let your thinking go astray of the path of your personal guidance system (PGS), it's as if you have taken another shuttle of the roughest, ugliest thread and started weaving with that. At that point, it doesn't even matter what your warp is, what your beliefs are, what your values are, or anything. Even though the strength is underneath, the actions of passing your shuttle through the warp, it affects the results you get. And this "fabric" represents the foundation out of which you will "cut" your life's design.

What is in Your Way, and Who are You Blaming?

Texture is a beautiful way of looking at your life and what you're creating, and also a great way to discover what is in your way of living your best life now. In fiber arts school, the most beautiful things we wove were almost like capes, but they had sleeves, so they were jacket capes. They were much more complicated but they were wonderful, and so worth the extra effort. What do you want to create? Are you passionate enough about creating your life masterpiece to be as magnificent as possible? Then you have to be practicing all the time, in the work of being aware of your thinking, and making conscious choices at all times.

I am going to use texture to look at another paradigm that often gets in the way of creating that beautiful piece of cloth from which you are crafting your life, and that is blame. Who are you blaming? Whose shuttle, if you will, are you picking up to throw? Is this the anger that you have towards your siblings, or your parents, or your workplace? What thoughts are you picking up? And who are you blaming? A way to let go of blame is forgiveness.

Forgiveness Allows You to Let Go and Move On

Why is it important that you practice forgiveness? If you don't, it's like taking your dream and planting it into toxic soil. What will be the results of that? The reason you need to forgive on an ongoing basis is that you need to continually be clearing things up all the time. It's like brushing your teeth once and thinking the job is done forever; you have to continually stay in that place of forgiveness. If you don't think you have anyone to forgive, then my guess is you're not breathing. All of us have to work on this; we're human. Somebody cut you off today, somebody turned you down for something, someone did something "to" you. All of this causes resentment within you. It's part of the human process. Not your true nature, but the status quo practice. You are the victim when you blame, and if you are the victim, you can't move forward. You must give up blame to experience your true nature.

Resentment and blame do not hurt the other person. If you're throwing the resentment (like the shuttle), you're the one who's getting hurt. You're the one messing up your own weaving. You're the one who's spending your energy holding on to resentment. I do believe that a lot of people's cancer is a result of some internal resentment and blame.

Creating a Pattern of Forgiveness and Building Texture

It's work. Work that *you* have to do. Nobody else can change you. One of the things I learned about sewing, weaving, and other fiber arts was to have enough patience to undo my mistakes. If I was weaving or knitting or sewing and noticed I made a mistake, instead of saying oh it's okay to leave it there, I had to have the patience to go back and take out the threads all the way back to that mistake. And then to make it right. That is not innate behavior; it is learned. In the same way, if I made a mistake in the past that can be corrected I go back to the beginning of that mistake and correct it as well as I can. In that way the texture of my life is again beautiful and harmonious and is moving in the direction from which I continue to craft my life.

> **"Every act is either an expression of love or a call for love, regardless of how unskillful it may appear."**
> - *A Course in Miracles*

Learning How to Forgive

A couple of years ago, I worked with a client who loved her father very, very much, but there were some things that had really bothered her as she was growing up. Among those, divorce and other personal disappointments. In the program she was in with me, I taught forgiveness work. One of the things that I talked about was how unskillful some people are. We talked about the concept of capacity. What is a person's capacity to be a good person, to be thoughtful, to make the right decisions? Everybody has their own capacity, a learned concept. It is embodied through their environment and experiences, such as what they learned from parents, teachers, and the media.

Let's think of capacity as a woven basket, with all of the experiences being the reeds that you use to create the basket. If that is capacity, that is all you have from which to respond. Most people think whatever basket they were given, they're stuck with. When they look at their basket, they don't realize those things that happened to them are actually the materials that make up their basket. And they don't consider that they can re-weave the basket. They just accept that it is their capacity. You can, however, change your capacity through forgiveness of others and forgiveness of self.

Use your frequency thermostat from the tool in Chapter 2. Think of the vibration of the thought that a person did something *to* you. That makes you the victim. When you are the victim, you cannot change. You are under the effect of the other person. But if you let go of blame, you are no longer the victim, and you can change things. One of the best ways to let go of blame is through forgiveness.

This young woman, the client I mentioned earlier, didn't know the backstory of her father's life. She didn't know why he acted the way he did sometimes. In realizing that somehow, his basket had been woven out of his own imperfect past, all of a sudden, she realized, "Oh, whatever that is, that's his backstory, and I don't need to know it." In that moment, she was able to let go of old resentments and forgive her father.

Loving Kindness Meditation and Forgiveness Song

There were some people living near our house, and they were selling drugs. One of my neighbors was talking to me about it. He is a big, burly guy, very sweet; but you don't want to be on the wrong side of him. He was saying how he would do something to these guys if he caught them in the act. I didn't want that kind of energy in my life either. I searched my tools and remembered about forgiveness. I used a Dalai Lama loving kindness meditation. A local artist had put it to a melody. Every time I passed by the drug dealers' house I sang to myself:

> May I be filled with loving kindness,
>
> May I be well,
>
> May I be peaceful and at ease,
>
> And may I be happy.

And then I would direct my attention toward the drug dealers' house and sing to them:

> May *YOU* be filled with loving kindness,
>
> May *YOU* be well,
>
> May *YOU* be peaceful and at ease,
>
> And may *YOU* be happy.

Then, in the deepest practice, in my mind, I put myself in the same circle as them in and sang:

> May *WE* be filled with loving kindness,
>
> May *WE* be well,
>
> May *WE* be peaceful and at ease,
>
> And may *WE* be happy.

"May *WE* be happy" was so incredibly powerful. Yes, that problem resolved itself. I could have stirred things up, I could have called my burly neighbor, I could have made things worse, but instead, I used loving kindness. That's the name of the song, "Loving Kindness." Words by the Dalai Lama adapted and sung by Karen Drucker from her album, *Songs of the Spirit 1* www.karendrucker.com

"Out beyond the ideas of wrongdoing and rightdoing, there is a field. I will meet you there."
- Rumi

Are you willing to meet me there? This is some really deep work, and it is transformational work.

Always ask yourself, "What is keeping me from my good, what is mine to do?"

Law of Forgiveness
~ Letting go of blame, and changing your perception.

"If you hold in your mind that someone has wronged you or has treated you unjustly, you cannot be free from your wrongdoings or injustice, so long as you hold that thought in your consciousness." - Raymond Holliwell, *Working With The Law*

"Human forgiveness is the process that frees us to live in the Eternal Now. It is the essential step before real spiritual growth can flourish." - Ernest Holmes, *The Science of Mind*

Tool: The Four Stages of Spiritual Conscious
by Michael Bernard Beckwith
(Used by permission)

Using the chart below, Stage 1 is where you feel like things happen **TO YOU**, and that you are at the effect of things around you.

Step 1.
In the bottom of column 1, you move out of the position and thoughts of being a victim and into Stage 2, **BY ME,** where you need to give up blame and shame.

Action:
As it mentions, one of the best ways to do this is forgiveness work. Not only those you feel victim to, but also yourself for however you

may have responded to the situation. Begin to shift your thinking by removing blame from the equation:

"I forgive people who I feel have wronged me and release all resentment."

"I am forgiving, loving, gentle, and kind to everyone."

"I acknowledge my part in the event and forgive myself completely."

Step 2.

Even when you feel someone has done something *to* you, if you take responsibility for your emotions and let go of that blame, you have the opportunity to make change. Even if something random happened and you were harmed in some way, if you cannot find a way to let it go, you will be stuck repeating it internally. As a victim, you remain the victim.

Action:

Claim your own wellbeing, or even the support of a higher power to free yourself of it:

"I love myself and all that I am, and all that I am not."

"It is my Nature to experience the best in life, and that includes how I care for myself."

Step 3.

Notice in Column 2, it says, "I can control my thoughts and my actions." With that approach, you can change the situations.

Action:

Use replacement thoughts and affirmations when you find yourself in blame:

"I choose to respond in a loving way."

"I am deserving of being treated kindly.

And my favorite: "The Divine has my back."

Etc.

Step 4.

Contemplate how you would respond differently if you came from this point of view. You can then take control of your life. Act from this place of knowing.

This chart has two more stages, but for now, start with practicing this first shift. I do teach the other stages in my work.

THE FOUR STAGES OF SPIRITUAL CONSCIOUSNESS
By Michael Bernard Beckwith

STAGE ONE	STAGE TWO	STAGE THREE	STAGE FOUR
To Me	By Me	Through Me	As Me
Victim	Law	Vessel	One
Forgiveness practices	Affirmations, Visualization, Vision Boards, Best case scenarios	Visioning Meditation Mindset of Openness, Receptivity, Beginners mind, Affirmative Prayer	Meditation, Visioning
The experience of having no control	The experience of the power to manifest	The experience of being a vessel or channel through which Spirit speaks and acts	The experience of Divine Oneness, Mystic Mind and of being One with Spirit
"Why does this always happen to me?"	"I can control my thoughts and my life"	"It is not I, but God, that does the work"	"I am one with God"
The opportunity to give up blame and shame	The opportunity to give up control and power	The opportunity to give up a sense of separation	The opportunity to experience limitless consciousness as Me

The Four Stages of Spiritual Consciousness is a guideline meant to provide a description of the evolutionary process, which itself is continually evolving. You may observe your life structures* expressing at different levels within these stages. They are dynamic, not linear or static.

CHAPTER 8
ALL IN PERSPECTIVE

Drawing perspective is taking a three-dimensional image and creating it as a two-dimensional image on a piece of paper and yet giving the perception of the three-dimensional image.

"If you're not as happy, healthy, and wealthy as you'd like to be, I urge you to step back and look at your situation from a different perspective. But don't just look at it in a general or superficial way; go further than you ever have before. Look beyond the reasons you've come up with for why you can't change or get what you want until you "see" a way to improve your current circumstances. Do it now, and prepare to rewrite your story."
- Bob Proctor

Nothing is Bad Until You Think It's Bad

There was this company that made shoes and they decided that they wanted to investigate what it was like to sell shoes in Africa. They sent off a salesman to go over to investigate and see what he found. He got over there, and he saw all of these people without shoes, and he sent back a message saying, "Stop production immediately. No one here wears shoes." Another shoe company had the same idea, so they sent their salesperson over. That person saw the same thing. However, he said, "Increase production. No one here wears shoes." So, how you view something is your perspective. Where are you standing in the picture? *Nothing is bad until you think it's bad.*

That goes for the boogeymen (paradigms) in your life. Although they challenge you, there are actually lessons within the boogeymen, usually teaching you what not to do. You can look for the good in your challenges and learn from them, to seek the lessons they have for you, and to use those pieces of wisdom as stepping stones. Remember the story of my dad? My business ended up taking a natural hiatus. And I was able to get my knee done and travel. Yes, it's sad that my parents have died. I miss them very much, but I will tell you, I am glad they are not alive during this pandemic.

I was taking a friend with me for an adventure in New York City. She had never been, and she was very excited. She borrowed my truck to pick up her things, and then we were going to head to the airport using the truck. She called me from a restaurant where she had been meeting a friend, and told me the truck had been stolen from the parking lot while she was eating.

I calmly asked her if she could get to my house with her stuff to go on the trip. She said yes, and I told her to call the Ministry of Prayer and get to my house. "You're not freaked out?" she asked. "There is nothing I can do about it now, and we have a plane to catch," I replied. Of course, I called my insurance company and then ordered a cab to the airport.

We had a grand time. When I got home, I had a call that they found my truck. Stripped of its nice sound system and speakers, a little bit of damage, but all of that caused it to be totaled. I actually got to keep the truck and got money from it being totaled, which allowed me to not only put a new stereo, but some safety features and upgrades. I could have spent time fussing about the truck, spoiling my trip to New York, but I managed to stay calm and enjoy myself. Nothing's bad until you think it's bad.

Look at a Problem from Multiple Viewpoints

Several years ago, I founded and ran a program for teens called NewClear Experiences. It was an explosion of new, clear thinking. I created a process called The Viewing Point. Whenever one of the kids bumped up against a concept or a personal issue inside or outside the program, I would hand the kid a piece of paper with the words "Viewing Point" on it, and have them define their problem. We would get into a circle, and the paper would be set in the middle. We'd go around the room and ask everyone to share their viewpoint on the issue. In order to get a variety of perspectives on this, I would assign some of them different characters, such as one would be a nun, one would be a judge, one would be a friend, one would be Mom, or sometimes even an alien, various things like that. This would allow the kid a chance to see other viewpoints, which added to their perception of the issue, and be able to make a more thought-out decision.

Take the opportunity to look at things from different perspectives. And then look again at your problem. First of all, you will find there are very many different types of perspectives, not that you accept their perspective, but you will be encouraged to look at things differently. This can take the extreme energy off of the problem and allow you to look at it less judgmentally or critically. This helps with you beginning to see your own solution, because in every problem, there is a solution.

One afternoon, I was in a swimming pool, and I saw a bug fall into the water. I wanted to help the little thing out. As I tried to rescue this bug, it totally freaked out. It didn't know I was trying to help it. It thought I was trying to harm it, so I couldn't get close. You can imagine the splash of water that went up over the side of the pool. It was pretty tumultuous, but there was a solution happening right then for that bug, and its life was saved. It's really hard to trust in situations when you see what could be called conflict, problem, or circumstances. How do you move through them?

When you apply beyond-the-box thinking and say to yourself, "Maybe, just maybe, this is what it looks like while it's all coming together," you open to a greater consideration of the event. What if you, like the bug in the water, are being rescued by the wave? What if this tumultuous time is clearing out your old perspectives to make way for you to become what you were born to be? This is what has happened to me during the pandemic. Say to yourself, "I don't know why, and I don't know how, but even this is moving me to living my life as a masterpiece."

The Gift of Perspective

Thoreau said, "The Universe is wider than our views of it. Direct your eye right inward and you'll find a thousand regions in your mind yet undiscovered. Travel them, and be an expert in home-cosmography." There's a word, right? Cosmography. That home inside of you takes you to the Infinite. There is nothing you can't create if you begin thinking beyond the box; Creative Thinking Expanded. The gift of perspective is what allows you to be the architect of your own future, the artist of your own masterpiece, rather than a victim of circumstances. You have the choice to perceive every situation, no matter how dire it seems to be (though, of course, you honor your human grief), in a positive and empowering light. You can choose to view the situation as disempowering. When you think of yourself in a disempowering way, what you are really doing is denying the Divine. You're saying that something that was created out of the Divine, and something that was created to express the Divine in a way that has never been expressed before, is not good enough. When you degrade yourself, or think that you are not good enough, or move in the direction of poverty or discord, you are out of harmony with the Greater Truth, and that's where the working gets hard.

So, what do you do with this? Guess what! There is wisdom in the boogeyman. Instead of turning around because you ran into the boogeyman again, you can step up and ask that boogeyman, "What do you have to teach me?" Everything is pulling you into your greatness, even your paradigms. It is only your perspective that determines the actions you take, and the results you get.

I was invited to work with a group of young soldiers in the Army. They were mostly in their early twenties, and almost all of them said they couldn't stand being in the Army. I said, "Then let's look at where you want to go when you finish your tour of duty." I helped them craft a vision for that. Then, I asked them, "How can you use the Army like your servant to get you to your dream?" This changed their perspective of where they are now and how it can lead them to their life design. They each came up with things toward which they could direct their Army career that would help them fulfill that dream. One wanted to be a secretary, so she decided to take all job offerings in her platoon that would help her learn the skills of being a secretary. They were also allowed to take community college classes, and another person was going to choose classes in finance and business, so she could run her own business when she got out. By the end of my time with them, there was a greater sense of finding value in their current situation.

Viewing the Past from a New Perspective Facilitates Self-Forgiveness

Jennifer Ashley Allen says, "You are not your actions. You are not a prisoner of your mistakes. It's a self-imposed prison when we hold onto guilt and shame. But the keys to escape lie within you. So, let go of the past. Forgive yourself. Learn from it and move on." Without self-forgiveness, you will be in a continuous loop of limiting conditions. You cannot create anything new and different that will create lasting results until you truly forgive yourself. For a review on forgiveness, see Chapter 7.

❦ ❦ ❦

> *Law of Abundance ~ Abundance is always present.*
> *We need to become the match.*
>
> "All that anyone will ever need or desire is already provided by Universal Abundance. This applies to everybody, not just some people." - Ernest Holmes
>
> "Turn the energy of your mind upon the ideas of plenty, love, happiness, joy, health, and they, in turn, will appear." - Raymond Holliwell

Tool: The Viewing Point

Perspective is the way we perceive a situation or challenge we are going through. Sometimes, we can have tunnel vision and can only see something from our own point of view. The viewpoint of others is for your consideration, not for them to make your decisions. It's just a tool to get out of your own limited thinking.

Let's practice creating a new narrative by looking at different points of view.

1. Choose a challenge or situation that you have strong feelings about.

   a. Think or write down the details from your own perspective.

   b. Notice words or phrases that come up as you think about it.

2. Now, using that same situation, think about it from another perspective. This could be a person involved in the situation with you or an objective observer.

3. Repeat this process two or three more times using different perspectives and ways of seeing the situation.

4. Reflect on any changes in the way you now think or feel about this situation after looking at it from several different perspectives. With this expanded view, choose what is true for you.

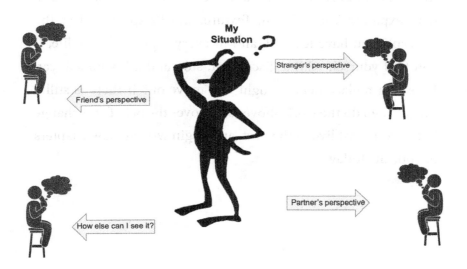

SUMMARY OF CRITIQUE

Critique has been about taking a look at what is in the way and how to change those thoughts or situations. This doesn't end by moving on to the next section of this book. This is probably the most important work to do over and over again. You have explored Value, Form, Texture, and Perspective. Use the concepts you have learned, and in every aspect of your life, if you find yourself with a discontent, stop and ask yourself, can I create a replacement thought and move on? If there is still a niggle, then do the work above to discover the belief and change it. Let your past live in the past, and begin writing new chapters of your life today.

PART THREE

CREATE:
BRINGING IT INTO REALITY

You are in the final phase. It is time to begin painting that masterpiece of your life. Remember to pay attention to your thoughts when I say this. It's the first thing to do when you move into the creating phase, and don't bring your old beliefs forward with you. If they come up, go back to Part 2 and stare them down. Put the tools you have learned thus far in designing and critiquing to work. Nothing will change until you change. And it takes repetition. Just because we have moved through the first two parts of this book, doesn't mean you don't keep practicing. Practice until it becomes your second nature, or better yet, make it your first nature.

Remember, the Divine is expressing itself through you. Make your life beautiful, make it creative, make it joyful! This is what life is meant to be. Here are the tools to guide you into creating your best life.

CHAPTER 9
IN BALANCE

"Happiness is not a matter of intensity,
but of balance, order, rhythm, and harmony."
- Thomas Merton

In a work of art, balance allows you to resonate with it, to enjoy it and be able to appreciate the work. Even if it evokes disturbing emotion, balance will be used to provoke that, as in asymmetrical balance. Balance or resonance is what you are looking for in life.

Balance, as a principle in life, is best understood through the Law of Reciprocity. Reciprocity is the flow between giving and receiving (not getting). When you are out of balance, it is either because you are more into giving than receiving or the other way around, or you feel some lack in your belief in yourself. That's when ego comes in; overcompensating for what is out of balance.

Beyond the Box is work that helps you move beyond your limited thinking. Although the past is considered, it is not the focus of the work. Beyond the Box starts at that point of understanding you are no longer a victim of circumstances and that you can take charge of your life. It is teaching you to use creative thinking, which is thinking thoughts you have never thought before, along with the expanded thinking, which is understanding and using the Universal Principles along with creative thinking.

Mastering the art of life is about balance. It's one of the core principles in the program. Have you ever noticed that you may be proficient in one arena of your life, and feel out of control in another? Time is often one of those challenging areas. Saying there's not enough time to do_____, or always running late, or putting off things of importance on your to-do list. These are examples of being out of balance in proportion to the other areas of your life. This is about striving for equilibrium.

Here is a quiz you can use to see where you might be out of balance in your life.

Answer **2** for <u>Yes, usually</u>, **1** for <u>Sometimes</u>, and **0** for <u>Not really</u>.

Balance Quiz

<u>Section 1 - Caring</u>   <u>Score</u>

    1. I am involved in community activities.   ___
    2. I recycle and conserve energy.   ___
    3. I brush my teeth and have good hygiene.   ___
    4. I care about people and things around me.   ___
    5. I am involved in the financial care of myself.   ___
                              Total   ___

<u>Section 2 - Contemplation</u>

    1. I relax or take quiet time 10 to 20 minutes every day.   ___
    2. I am at peace with myself.   ___
    3. I don't bite or pick my nails.   ___
    4. I don't feel overly stressed from day to day.   ___
    5. I stop throughout the day and pay attention to my breathing.   ___
                              Total   ___

<u>Section 3 - Sensing</u>

    1. I take walks in nature.   ___
    2. I give myself treats or presents.   ___
    3. I like being with people.   ___
    4. I avoid extremely noisy areas.   ___
    5. At times, I like to be alone.   ___
                              Total   ___

<u>Section 4 - Eating</u>

    1. I drink fewer than five soft drinks per week.   ___
    2. I avoid fats and sugar in my diet.   ___

3. I avoid fast foods. ___
4. I eat only when I'm hungry. ___
5. I eat two to five fresh fruits and vegetables a day. ___

Total ___

Section 5 - Exercise

1. I climb stairs, rather than take the elevator. ___
2. I have an exercise plan and follow it. ___
3. I enjoy stretching and moving my body. ___
4. I learn new ways of caring for my body. ___
5. I pay attention to how my body feels. ___

Total ___

Section 6 - Feeling

1. I allow myself to experience a full range of emotions. ___
2. I have several close friends. ___
3. I express my feelings for others. ___
4. It is easy for me to laugh. ___
5. I feel okay about crying when I'm sad. ___

Total ___

Section 7 - Thinking

1. It is easy for me to concentrate. ___
2. I notice when my thoughts are influenced by things around me. ___
3. I am creative. ___
4. I can find a solution to most problems. ___
5. I know when I am judging things around me. ___

Total ___

Section 8 - Playing and Working

1. I enjoy expressing myself through art, dance, sports, etc. ___
2. I am satisfied with my abilities to work. ___
3. I have people around me who support my playfulness. ___
4. I sometimes allow myself to do nothing. ___
5. I have at least one hobby or interest for pleasure. ___

Total ___

Section 9 - Communicating.

1. I consider what I am going to say before I say it. ___
2. I communicate clearly with friends and family. ___
3. I am a good listener. ___
4. I enjoy good conversations with others. ___
5. I admit my mistakes when I am aware of them. ___

Total ___

What were your scores in each section? The tool at the end will help you utilize them. This is not about accomplishing the 'very best' in each one. You are looking for overall balance. At times in my life, such as when I told my son I had been around teenagers all week and he was feeling neglected, I was giving more attention to my career than my family life and my health. I can see now that being out of proportion in one area of my life led to some of my health challenges. Also, I am a very social person and the Law of Sacrifice comes into play. Sometimes, you need to let go of some things, such as social time, in order to accomplish a goal. That's not always my first choice, but sometimes, I need to do that to create balance in my life. And on the other hand, sometimes, you need to let go of time working, to have social time.

Taking Stock of Your Answers

Notice the highest and the lowest scores. This is not to get the highest numbers. You want to bring all of these things into balance, within range of each other. If you have a really high number in one section, and a really low number in another section, you may need to put less emphasis on the high activities (you probably have those well in hand), and more time into the lower numbers, bringing everything into balance.

Types of Balance

Looking to the art principles, there are several kinds of balance. There are symmetrical, asymmetrical, and radial. Symmetrical balance is where all sides are evenly weighted. Asymmetrical balance is where, although the space may be divided up differently, there still is a sense of balance. For example, if there is a larger space that is open and vast, and a small section with lots of texture and visual weight, the two areas can draw about the same amount of attention. Radial balance centers around a central point, and the design radiates out like a mandala. And all of these design definitions can also apply to your life or to a project.

Symmetrical: is my work balanced by my fun? Or, asymmetrical: is the intensity of my work balanced by greater attention to a more relaxed area of my life? And radial: is there a center that influences all of the aspects of my life?

Clutter is a common problem for many people. Various types of balance can be applied to clutter. When I work on projects, or even when I'm producing my coaching calls, I work in what many people would call a cluttered environment. I have several books open on my desk and resources from my files flying around. For me, it's part of my creative process. I think about this idea of asymmetrical balance. This creative chaos doesn't usually bother me, but when it does get to the point of bothering me, I do stop and clean it up. Remember this is also about balance in the arena of time, so I have to consider the amount of time that I have to do these things in the course of the week. This is how it works for me. A pile here, a notebook open there, and then things start getting stacked on them. That's when I say to myself, "Whoa, back up here," and get myself organized as quickly as possible. If I balance that to the rest of my life, it doesn't matter which kind of balance I use. I do, however, need to pay attention to make sure the clean-up process stays within the limits of time I have for business and not let it leak into taking care of myself, or my family time.

I have always loved cheetahs. I find I have a similar quality to them, sprint and rest. As I am getting older, the rest and recovery time is getting longer. I was on a retreat in Hawaii, and we were swimming with the turtles. I started looking at that turtle energy. I said, "You know what? I'm going to take on that turtle energy, which is the pull and glide." The cheetah habit still works for some things, and the pull and glide works for others. Either way, I get to pay attention to my overall balance.

Understanding the Law of Vibration

Remember in Chapter 2 about Line; in creating the life you love living you first must have a feeling that matches what you would love. This is where most people get confused with the Law of Attraction versus the Law of Vibration. Now, *The Secret* talked about the Law of Attraction, and taught that if you create an image of it, then you will be able to manifest it. Many people created vision boards and waited for things to happen. For the people who tuned in vibrationally, the feeling of it, it did happen for them. But the piece of this that is so important, and it is the primary principle here, is the Law of Vibration. You have to *feel* it before you see it. You have to *be* it within not only your imagination, but within the very cells of which you are made before it comes *to* you. The principle of balance is actually going to help you create the foundation to bring your life design into the world.

Consider how the wind works. The wind doesn't blow; it is pulled into the low-pressure front. This is about having a feeling of what you want to become: *I am the woman who expresses brilliantly in the world.* That's a vibrational frequency. You may feel you first have to know how you will get there. That idea of needing to know how is actually the main thought that stops you not only from accomplishing your masterpiece, but in even dreaming it. The Universe has *so* many more different "hows," and when you try to squeeze out the answer through your little thinking mind, it limits the quantum field out there, and you begin to limit yourself and the possibilities that the Universe wants to provide.

Now, "steps in the direction" are very different from the how. Taking a step in the direction toward what you would love creates an action within the quantum field that notifies the Universe, the Divine, that this is the direction in which you are moving, and it creates a pull toward your vision. I was coaching a woman who asked me if it would get in the way of her life design if she took a job at Walgreen's. I asked her if that would help her towards her dream. "Well, it will help me pay my rent." I said, "Yes, take the job!" We all take many steps that may not even look like they are moving us in the right direction. This is a good time to use your PGS. But even with baby steps, you can climb Mt. Everest. Many baby steps can take you to your dream, but pay attention to the *thoughts* that can take you in a different direction. If so, stop those thoughts, and don't just walk, *run* back in the direction toward your life design!

At the end of my son's second year of college, the university closed down. At first, it seemed devastating, and he was angry. But, the professors at the school realized they needed to build their portfolios at that time and decided to make a film. My son was invited to work on it. Then, my son thought beyond the box of just working on a film. He asked us if he could use a semester's tuition money to help produce the movie. When we look at what he was able to do, gain more than classroom education, we said yes. He was able to turn his personal disaster around and have a beautiful outcome that took him so much closer to what he wants in the world, and I am so happy for him. He could have stayed in his anger and left to come back home and sulk. He had already taken all of the necessary filmmaking classes. But, he remained with his professors to work on the movie, learned so much more, and had a great experience. It won many festival awards. He now has credits in IMDb for making movies as a producer, designing special effects, and various other things.

Let's take a deeper dive into vibrational frequency. Generally, people's brains think in pictures. When you hear the word "door," you don't see the letters D-O-O-R. I imagine a purple door; you'll probably see whatever your front door is. You manifest through your image as well. Your thoughts create images, and the images move through your passion, your emotion, and that is what's going to propel your idea into you taking action. Then, just like the wind, everything you need (such as people, resources, and new ideas), moves to support you to make that happen and come into being. As long as you get out of the way. That's how these principles work. That's the principle of the Law of Vibration. This is why you write out a very clear and detailed vision encompassing all senses, a full visual sketch of your life, to get your brain to produce the frequency match, and why you read it every day, as if it has already taken place. This keeps the vision of your dream clear and the vibration high.

Law of Reciprocity
~ *What goes around comes around.*

"For every visible form, there is an invisible counterpart. This means that what we receive corresponds to what we imagine and believe we can receive, the law of Mental Equivalents. This is also the Golden Rule: that what we do to others will be done also to us, the Law of Cause and Effect." - Ernest Holmes

Tool: Wellness Tool

Use the numbers you scored in each section and fill in the grid. Look for the area that is the average:

Now see which ones are high and which ones are low. Take the lower ones and set some goals to raise those. Take the higher ones and think of ways you can take some focus or time away (in a healthy way) to bring it closer to your average. Everyone will have a different place that is their average.

Wellness Quiz Example

EXAMPLES	Section Scores									
Sections	1	2	3	4	5	6	7	8	9	10
Caring										✗
Contemplation							✗			
Sensing							✗			
Eating							✗			
Exercise				✗			→			
Feeling								✗		
Thinking								✗		
Playing & Working									✗	
Communication									✗	

THE AVERAGE ↗

Wellness Quiz Tool

EXAMPLES	Section Scores									
Sections	1	2	3	4	5	6	7	8	9	10
Caring										
Contemplation										
Sensing										
Eating										
Exercise										
Feeling										
Thinking										
Playing & Working										
Communication										

CHAPTER 10
YOU'VE GOT RHYTHM

**"Life is about rhythm. We vibrate, our hearts are pumping blood.
We are a rhythm machine. That's what we are."
- Mickey Hart, drummer**

I attended a retreat with the intention to rest and sleep and rejuvenate, as well as deepen my spiritual experience. It was a luxury hotel, and I had a room with a patio on the pool level, and I could walk out to take a swim or a hot tub. The bed had a fluffy white duvet, and was so delicious to snuggle into. On my first morning to sleep in, I was awakened very early in the morning by the people next door making so much noise, laughing and giggling! "Didn't they know it was very important for me to get my sleep?" I stopped myself, and I realized it was a room for a bride and her bridesmaids to prepare for her wedding day. It was a very special day for them. Then, I realized my initial response to this chatter next door was part of my deeper work: "Oh, I can change my thinking." This led me to revisit the memory of the beautiful experience on my wedding day. I had all of my bridesmaids over, with a hairdresser to do our hair, and over brunch, I gave them all pretty spritzer bottles to use for perfume or rosewater. And I recalled the joy I had shopping for that special gift for each one of them. My mood shifted, and even though the chatter was still going on in the next room, it turned into a lullaby as I reminisced about my own wedding day. I transformed my experience. You can transform your thoughts. You can choose the rhythm that you want to be dancing to.

You are the composer of your life, the artist. Look around you: what you have in your life, you have crafted. And just as you crafted it (mostly unconsciously up to this point), with awareness through the tools of creative thinking expanded, you can craft a new life.

For my beautiful wedding (before flash mobs), my husband and I took lessons, and we had someone help us choreograph a dance to a special song for us. I have always loved to dance, but Jerry was not always comfortable, and I grew up with "free form" dancing! We found someone to teach us, and we learned a new rhythm. But how did we get that rhythm in us? Repetition. Repetition. Repetition. Doing it over and over again.

Mickey Hart, the drummer for the Grateful Dead, said, "Life is about rhythm. We vibrate, our hearts are pumping blood. We are a rhythm machine. That's what we are." Now, think about the concept of vibration. You are a rhythm machine. Your breathing, your heart pumping, your cells regenerating, those are all functions of the human body, and they set a rhythm that dictates and runs your physical life. Just as that's true for the physical, it is also true for your mental and spiritual life. And for manifesting in your life, it's all about the rhythm within you.

Think of music. Music is a really great way to see how rhythm affects us. Also called vibration. I used to sing "Hush little baby, don't say a word, Mama's gonna buy you a mockingbird..." to my son. And then, in the shower in the morning, I would sing, "You've got to get up every morning with a smile on your face and show the world all the love in your heart!" (from *Beautiful*, by Carole King). So those are two different rhythms, and then there's the dirge: dun - dun - dun - dun - dadun - dadun - dadun. Or the rhythm of swing, or the cha-cha. You can identify the different types of music because of the rhythm. And if you look at artwork, you can see rhythm in the composition. Does the piece have a nice beat to it? Is it uplifting, and does it help you feel good? That sets a tone for your vibrational frequency.

How Changing Your Thinking Can Change Your Feeling and Your Experience

Rhythm is so important for you in creating and bringing your work into the world. Think of the rhythm when you continue worrying about money. What kind of rhythm is that? Every time you worry about money, the money just cha cha's right out the door! That's the rhythm you are painting on your canvas of life! Every time you have doubt, whatever you are doubting eludes you. Consider this quote by Emerson: "Stand guard at the portal of your mind." You cannot let anything unlike what you want to create cross over your mind. Not even in the moment of being disappointed or having something go astray, or awry. You may feel disappointed, but in such a moment, say to yourself, "Ah! But I'm going to change this. I'm going to change my experience of this." Then, repeat as often as necessary.

This is how you create your life by design, rather than by default. Wallace Wattles states: "There is Thinking Stuff from which all things are made, and which in its original state, permeates, penetrates, and fills the interspaces of the Universe. A thought in this substance produces the thing that is imagined by the thought." A thought in the Thinking Stuff creates after its kind. An acorn does not produce a stalk of corn. The doubt is like expecting corn and getting an oak tree. Doubt thoughts do not create your intended outcome.

Remember the formula in Chapter 6: Thought, Emotion, Action, Results? It not only helps you pay attention to what you want to change, but it is a method that you can use to create your masterpiece. It is the same process that I used to create the workbook *The Creative Way in 5 Minutes a Day*. Here is how I applied that formula:

Every weekday morning for three months, I sat at my dining room table, often with an assistant, and here was my method:

<u>**My Thought**</u>: To create an adult coloring book.

<u>**My Emotion**</u>: Was passion. This was my masterpiece of this time, and I had excitement and joy.

<u>**My Action Step**</u>: Envisioning the completed workbook. Defining three steps I could take each day to move forward on the project.

<u>**My Results**</u>: Three months later, it was listed on a site and ready for market. This was not my normal rhythm before I had this inspiration. But my passion, my knowingness, was enough for me to create a new rhythm.

Once the workbook was created, I continued to use this formula to develop my other programs. See the list in Other Resources for further information and links.

> **Law of Success ~ by our nature, we are successful.**
>
> "The Law is our supply. It is our Divine Nature to be successful."
> - Raymond Holliwell

Tool: Switch Your Thinking
(See Offerings – 4 Success Tools)

There are two ways to switch your thinking.

1. When you can catch yourself in thoughts that lead you away from your life design or your core values, such as a judgement or opinion. (Remember my story of the bride getting ready?) This is a time to pause and choose to switch your thinking. For opinions that don't match your direction in your life design, look for some opposite thought. "Those girls in the next room are ruining my morning" to "It reminds me of my wedding day."

2. When you are just going down the slippery slope of negative thinking, or putting yourself down. For negativity or self-criticism, have some generic thoughts to replace fault-finding thoughts. In the Flying Leap Story, I used "I am well." You can use things such as: "I love myself, just the way I am, and just the way I'm not." Or, "I align myself with positive thoughts." Or, you could even say, "I am a good person." Get creative, think of ways to support yourself, as you would a dear one in your life. Most people would never talk to anyone the way they do to themselves in their heads.

Imagine a light switch. Even hear the click and Switch Your Thinking.

CHAPTER 11
MAIN EMPHASIS

"The creative power within us makes us into
the image of that which we give our attention."
- Wallace Wattles in *The Science of Getting Rich*

The Science of Getting Rich was published in 1910. At the time it was being written, people were realizing that thoughts create experience. Wallace Wattles called it "The Creative Power." You are creative in how you use your thoughts with the aid of creative thinking expanded. You are a receptacle for thoughts to come in and then things to be produced out of that thought. I want to remind you about The Law of Gestation. Just like a seed in the soil, you must nurture that seed with the right soil, water, and sun. It does take time. And even though you may get impatient, that's a good thing. Imagine, what if your thoughts became your reality before you had a chance to consider them? Some of your thoughts would cause disaster, but if you find yourself using repetition to imbed new thinking, it is like vetting the new thinking. It gives you time to be sure it is what you choose.

Experiencing What Is

You are the infinite presence in expression; that's what life is here for, to be the method by which the Divine experiences itself. Why would the Universe or the Divine (whatever you choose to call it) want us to experience anything other than peace, joy, and creativity? There is, of course, sadness in our lives, death of loved ones, loss of our security, and physical challenges. The deaths of my parents were very sad. There were moments I didn't even feel like I could breathe. I went through the grief, and I felt deep sadness, and yet, it was one of the richest times of my life. I was feeling life. I was feeling death. I was feeling the aliveness of being in my awareness work. Wallace Wattles says, "The creative power within us makes us into the image of that to which we give our attention." You are a receptacle, a machine; it is your purpose to create. What you learn from this work is that you get to choose what you create, but that can only happen with awareness.

You can wake up to, and begin choosing, these specific things that operate through you in the creative receptacle inside of you. How you do that is through emphasis, through giving your attention to something.

Being Grateful

"One way to create positive emphasis in your life is to practice gratefulness. When you begin your thoughts with gratitude for what you have, you develop a strong self-confidence and strengthen your ability to change your disasters into blessings." (from *The Creative Way in 5 Minutes a Day*). Make gratitude the emphasis in your life. And there's a deeper sense here. When you start your thoughts with gratitude just for being, it becomes a deeper sense of thankfulness. Just gratitude. Just *being* grateful.

Seven Truths to Deepen your Sense of Gratitude (adapted from *The Science of Getting Rich* by Wallace Wattles)

1. If your gratitude is strong and constant, the reaction in formless substance will be strong and continuous; the movement of the things you want will be always toward you.

2. You cannot exercise much power without gratitude, for it is gratitude that keeps you connected with power.

3. To fix your attention on the best is to surround yourself with the best, and to become the best.

4. The creative power within us makes us into the image of that which we give our attention.

5. The grateful mind is constantly fixed upon the best.

6. The reaction of gratitude upon one's own mind produces faith ... to give thanks continuously.

7. And because all things have contributed to your advancement, you should include all things in your gratitude.

Tithing is a principle of gratitude. We hear of it from the Bible, but it goes across the board. In most all religions, there's a sense of giving to your spiritual source. That's what tithing means, and it relates to the word tenth. One-tenth, or ten percent. Now, why one-tenth works, I don't know. I believe it's because it causes a bit of a stretch. A little bit outside of your comfort zone, but probably not enough to wig you out or to make you freak out because it's too much to give. But I've taken a deeper dive into understanding tithing, and it truly is about being in gratitude. It is a way that you can show gratitude and be in gratitude, to be serving that which you are grateful for, where you get your spiritual support. It could be a church, it could be a person, it could be a musician. A friend of mine was so spiritually inspired by a famous musician, she sent her tithe to that person. So, you can tithe to things that are of a spiritual nature to you, that feed you. Though the formula is that you give ten percent to tithing, it doesn't have to be ten percent to get started.

This is different from giving to places or people that you care about and you are giving to them because they are in need, such as animal rescues or homeless shelters. Think of the difference between the thought frequency of just giving out of gratitude, rather than to places of need. Although a kind gesture, it still is based on seeing things broken or not right. Giving to your spiritual source is totally out of gratitude and feeling whole in yourself. If you don't feel you have a source, think of who or what you are grateful for: my husband and I tithe to Gratefulness.org, or I often tithe to a teacher beyond my tuition, out of gratitude.

This is a story of tithing in my life, and how it worked for me and this whole sense of gratitude. I was accepted into the graduate school of my choice, Claremont Graduate School (now University). It was one of the top art schools in the nation, and not cheap at thirty thousand dollars a semester. I had no savings, no job as I went off to school, and my family was not in a position to support me. What I had was faith. Faith both in myself and in a higher power. It was accompanied by focus/emphasis and action. I did everything I could, I applied for all grants and scholarships and work study, I got a job as a waitress right away, and I took the director of the art department to lunch to glean his wisdom. I left no stone unturned, just like Genevieve Behrend says in *Your Invisible Power*, "Leave no stone unturned when you believe that you are moving in the direction of something, you do everything you know how to make it happen."

I got a small fifteen hundred dollar scholarship. Think about how far *that* would go when each semester was thirty thousand dollars. Still, I took a hundred and fifty dollars to tithe on the small grant I had received. I knew the power and importance of tithing, of gratitude, and had already been practicing it. I was assisting at a church in a youth group at the time. I went to the youth group to help out on a Sunday, and I had my one hundred fifty dollar check. At that time, I didn't even know how I was going to pay the full tuition, I didn't know how I was going to make my rent, and yet had to move into a place both of faith and of gratitude.

<hr/>

And when the offering basket came around, I held my check, and I felt like a court jester, and I kind of laughed, like, "Okay, Universe, let's see how you return this to me tenfold." I didn't give to get something back, but I knew that's the principle, give purely out of gratitude and it'll come "pressed down and overflowing." That is a tenfold return. I gave it out of deep-felt gratitude. I was *so* grateful. I had faith.

Three days later, I got a letter from the Claremont Graduate School that said, "Due to the recommendation of the faculty in the Art Department of Claremont Graduate School, you have been awarded a fifteen thousand dollar grant. Now we're talking! Thank you, Universe! So why was it a hundred times, instead of ten times? I don't know. Except there was just this deep sense of faith and knowing, and almost like the universe wanted to laugh back with me, and say, "Yes, this really does work!" You can ask the universe to prove this to you, and you don't have to start with large amounts. You don't have to start with ten percent. You can even start with two percent, whatever is just above your comfort zone, until you see the increase happening. If it is sincere, it will show up to you proportional to how much gratitude is in that giving.

In Giving, You Place Emphasis on What is Important to You

Money is not the only thing that is tithed. You tithe your time and your talent, as well as your money. Tithing your time means volunteering somewhere, helping out. A friend of mine passed away, and wanting to help and honor my friend, I began driving her partner and her dog to the vet every two weeks to get the dog's treatment on her hind legs. That's one way I give my time. And as for tithing of my talent, I share my art or volunteer my services to some cancer and other programs. You want to give your time and your talent, as well as your money. These are some examples of how to pay attention to what you want to pay attention to.

Changing Limiting Belief Systems

What you believe influences that which you find yourself emphasizing in your life, and tend to focus attention upon. Often, your actions and patterns are based on deep-seated beliefs that you don't even realize are within you. I've talked about this effect a couple times, but it's always good to revisit. How do you change it, if you don't even know what the beliefs are? There is therapy, which can be very helpful if you feel overrun by your past. In the beginning, you do some self-discovery, but eventually, you look for the current discontent, and determine what you would love, instead. To do this, you can also use your life sketch (or life design) as a guide: is my discontent taking me off course to reach my vision, and if so, how can I readjust?

We used the five questions in the design phase. We did this to help you see if your life design is worthy of your time. I find these questions not only help with designing your vision, but also with creating it. Ask these five questions when you come to a crossroad, to help you determine which direction is helping you manifest your life design.

Ask Yourself:
- Does it give me life?
- Does it align with my core values?
- Does it cause me to grow?
- Do I need a higher power?
- Is there good in it for others?

Remember the fisherman story? He was limiting what he caught and took home based on his frying pan. What habits do you just continue to do, without even knowing the benefit of them, or where they came from? What frying pan are you limiting yourself to? Now, that's the question to ask yourself. Maybe you could catch bigger fish, you could fillet it in a certain way, or you could get a new pan, find other different options.

Notice What Your Attention is on

I want to share a quotation often attributed to Albert Einstein. He says, "Everything is energy, and that's all there is. Match what you want, and you cannot help but get that reality. It can be no other way. This is not philosophy. This is physics."

So, the greatest physicist in our history knew that if you match the frequency of the reality you want, you cannot help but get that reality. There can be no other way.

You want you to put your emphasis on what you love, and what you want to create, and you need to be constantly paying attention to your thoughts and what your thoughts are that you want to bring into the world.

Law of Gratitude
~ Gratitude is a vibration that will
allow all that you desire to come to you.

"The soul that is always grateful serves in closer touch with Spirit." - Wallace Wattles

Affirmation: "Fill me with gratitude for all You give. May I be a vehicle for You wherever I go. May I be grateful for every blessing and know your abundance as my Own Self. Open me to my own inner divinity and awaken me from the sleepwalk of being 'only' human." - Tosha Silver, *It's Not Your Money*

Tool: *"Gratitudes and Proud Ofs"*

Create a daily gratitude practice; there are many to choose from.

Here is one that I use, both as a daily practice and as a beginning of any work I do with clients.

1. Think of something you are Grateful for. This could be:

   a. I am grateful for my loving sister, who baked cookies for me!

   b. I am so grateful for the rain that we needed so badly!

   c. I am so grateful that my friend Heather called me yesterday to catch up!

2. Think of something that you are proud of in yourself. This is an important practice if you are to begin recognizing your own assets. You are often proud of others (your children and loved ones), but this is about you! This could be:

   a. I am so proud that I was able to finish my report completely and on time!

   b. I am proud of my patience when I support my children in their Zoom classes!

   c. I am proud of myself for sticking with my decision to get up a half hour earlier to meditate and have alone time.

CHAPTER 12
COMPLETE COMPOSITION: BRINGING IT ALL TOGETHER

"Our life is composed greatly from dreams, from the unconscious, and they must be brought into connection with action. They must be woven together."
- Anaïs Nin

Composition is when an artist arranges the different elements of an artwork, so as to bring those elements into a harmonious relationship with one another. This is where you bring it all together and take a good look at the whole picture. You, as the artist creating your life masterpiece, will think not just out of the box, but beyond the box. You will do the fine tuning, knowing how to use Creative Thinking Expanded.

When you look at a painting you love, you may not know why you love it. It is a feeling. This is the same thing you can do in looking at your life. Think of it as a painting of its own. Are you satisfied with your life? Where do you want to go next? Do you want to refine some of the specific aspects, such as forming a vision for your life? Or building up the set-point? Perhaps your goal is remembering to be grateful for all things as a whole. How can you create the greatest composition for your life?

You are the artist of your own life. And you have a Masterpiece, like DNA, that is yours to bring into the world. At a certain point, you can decide the composition of your life. I have been in human potential work for a very long time. I know I have changed the lives of hundreds of people, and through changing their lives, it has gone out into the world exponentially. And yet, as I looked at the composition of my life, I never felt it was complete. I searched for what was mine to give. I serve my clients all the time. Yet, I couldn't find anyone who could help me to get down to the very depths of what was mine to give, what was the light at the center. I defined the problem, or the discontent, really well every time I went to consult another professional.

I would start by telling them I have been in a spiral my whole life, since I was out of high school, retelling the story over and over again. I had three main longings. Number one: making art. Then realizing what was missing, which was number two: my gift of helping people. And number three: trying to find a way to connect the two. So, I had three dilemmas, cycling over and over again, and I still felt discontent. Here is an example of this: before our son was born, I was absolutely sure I wanted to be a full-time thriving artist. And I left no stone unturned. I was building a reputation, and art was all I wanted to do, except to start a family. I was a runner-up for a county-wide competition for an artist in residency position, based on my art. I was paying attention to this dilemma, recreating it every time I told the story.

After reaching out to so many professionals to help me bring my grand masterpiece forward, I stopped. I was confused. I felt like I had lost sight of who *I* was. I had believed, as they advised me, that I was doing my masterpiece by following their recommendations. Yet, with every career change, I felt incomplete.

Then, the pandemic arrived. And I was left with myself. I chose to use the time to turn within. I did call upon a couple of professionals who have the ability to evoke from me what is mine to do, rather than directing me or assuming they know my answer. During this time of introspection, I used my own art process to draw, and that really helped me experience deeper insights into my discontents. So, I drew from my intuition, combined with the guidance of the people I consulted. I let the images that crystalized in my drawings speak to me. For years, I had been drawing in this way, my feelings, my challenges. As an art therapist, I had guided many clients to draw and explore and find answers to their challenges. But, I also met lots of resistance of clients to the drawing process. Some clients or potential clients would say they couldn't draw. Others would say they couldn't figure out *what* to draw.

I belong to a healing group, and during meetings I started drawing other people's questions, pain, and even solutions. It isn't a part of the group activity, but as I listened to people sharing, I found myself drawing the same way I have been doing for myself for a long time. I take in much more deeply what they're saying, and "hear" beyond their words. I gave the drawings to my fellow group members, and they found profound healing in them.

As I continued to glean insight from my drawings, I shared them with others. They were astonished at the beauty, but also the depth of my drawings. The light turned on. Finally, I had the three dilemmas marriageable to one another, and it's a graceful fit. I could draw these intuitive wisdom drawings and guide people to use them in their self-discovery. Part of this insight was also an acceptance of my intuitive ability. Why hadn't I thought of that before? If I drew for others, but let them use the image to evoke insights, I could reach more people. An added benefit is that now, here I am, both artist and coach. I am now making art *and* helping people. I had always shied away from trusting my greater gifts of my connection with the Divine and my intuition. This is my composition, and it is beyond the box. And now, ideas of other possibilities are flowing.

If you've had times of feeling you've "arrived," but are still feeling discontent, it's probably because you are not done yet; there is still something longing to emerge through you. Perhaps what you've done before was meant to be built upon. So, don't throw away your discontent. Mine was speaking to me all along. It is just letting you know you haven't yet found the key to your grand masterpiece.

From *The Creative Way in Five Minutes a Day* workbook, in the second paragraph of Composition it says, "Composition is looking at the whole picture, and seeing if you're satisfied with all the elements or principles of design you have learned. This is the same thing you can do in looking at your life. Think of it as a painting of its own. Are you satisfied with your life? Where do you want to go next? Do you want to refine some of the specific aspects, such as forming your life design? Or building up the set-point? Perhaps your goal is remembering to be grateful for all things as a whole. How you can create the greatest composition for your life is to, as Mary Morrissey says, 'Look into our longings and discontents, as they will give us clues.' We look for the remedy to our discontents, as well as our longings, and from this, we create our template for our life composition."

Your Longings and Discontents Will Help You Create Your Composition

So, the importance of composition, as it says above, is that composition is really another tool for asking yourself: where is my discontent? And what am I longing for? This is an amazing tool to use in your life. What is your discontent? And what are you longing for? And this will help you, like when you're looking at a painting. For example, I have a painting that I've been working on. I keep putting it up in my painting class week after week, and everybody says it looks finished, it looks fine, but there's something in it that keeps bothering *me*, so does it matter that everybody else says it's fine? In considering their opinion I get really clear. No. *I* have discontent. What is my longing? My longing is to do with the balance of the painting; I feel it needs to be a little more balanced. And that's how *you* get to assess your life. The Divine in you has sent everything here to support you in being the greatest masterpiece it has ever created. Yes, everything, as hard as it is to see sometimes. But why would it do anything different? And it takes awareness of this deeper work, to, as Wattles says, "…think Truth regardless of appearance." This is Creative Thinking Expanded, this is thinking beyond the box, this is creating *your* box.

Law of Wholeness
~ We are expressions of the Divine.

"Spirit is a transcendent, perfect Whole that contains and embraces all seeming opposites. As human beings, we have free will and can show what we experience, whether it be positive or negative." - Ernest Holmes

Exercise:

Think back on an event that you have had where everything came together. It is good if it has visual interest, as your mind thinks in pictures.

Form this into one simple idea or sentence, and write it down.

Make sure this sentence is at a high frequency vibration!

Use this whenever you remember at a time you want to shift the frequency of your thought.

Examples:

Painting sunflowers in France

Walking in Hyde Park

Holding hands with my beloved in Armstrong Woods

Walking up the steps to receive my diploma.

SUMMARY OF CREATE

What would your life look like if all of this came true? It can. And it will. But, it is work. And as Wallace Wattles said, "To think according to appearance is easy; to think Truth regardless of appearance is laborious…" But it's worth it, and it gets easier the more you practice it.

And there is other good news. You don't have to do it alone. In fact, you can't do it alone. Remember Question #4? Does it require a higher power? That means you aren't alone. You may think you are, and if so, go back to the part on Critique and practice some more. This entire book is a guide to use continually to help you create your own box, and continue thinking beyond even that box.

How lovely is the Masterpiece of You!

ABOUT THE AUTHOR

Christi Corradi takes a generous, heart-centered approach to life, embracing each day with gusto and passion, and living the principles she teaches. Seeing life as an expansive canvas for creativity, she loves helping people express their own personal masterpiece — the manifestation of the best version of themselves.

Through her life-transforming program Mastering The Art of Life, Christi guides others to harness universal laws that sustain positive personal change. She uses proven self-discovery methods that open her clients to their infinite potential, inner faith, and self-love, while stopping limiting self-doubt and fear.

Her most recent approach to guiding personal growth and fulfillment is Intuitive Wisdom Drawing Sessions, where she taps into her intuition and art skills to help people find where they are stuck, find their own answers, step into their potential — and live their wildest dreams.

Life is fun and meant to be celebrated! Christi Corradi is the author of *The Creative Way in 5 Minutes a Day*, a program to awaken creative thinking with a daily practice. She is an international speaker and leads transformational small groups to foreign countries for fun and fulfillment.

Christi brings more than three decades in the field of personal development as an Art Therapist, Certified Life Mastery Consultant, and award-winning Transformational Life Coach. She lives with her family in the San Francisco North Bay. She is a world traveler and has been to over 35 countries. She also sells and exhibits her artwork.

If you would like to work with Christi or find out more, visit: MasteringTheArtOfLife.com/BeyondTheBook

OFFERINGS BY CHRISTI CORRADI

Sketch Your Life Session

You don't need to live a life limited by your current paradigms and beliefs. In this a 30-minute session Christi helps you create an outline of the life you would love to live, and steps to get there.

https://maol.as.me/Sketch

Intuitive Wisdom Sessions

Have you ever wanted a crystal ball to consult about your life? Well, here's your chance to see inside yourself with crystal clarity. A 60-minute session during which Christi draws an intuitive image while you talk about a discontent in your life. The process guides you to discover your own answers.

https://masteringtheartoflife.com/wisdom/

4Success Toolkit

Excuse Me button
Round Tuits
Erase 4Success
My Frequency Thermostat
Switch 4Success

https://masteringtheartoflife.com/product-category/tangible-tools/

The Creative Way 3-month program

DESIGN – The first three months are The Creative Way. At first your vision will be like a sketched outline. As the program progresses and you go deeper, more details will reveal themselves to you. You'll learn how to use Universal Laws and practices to envision your dream life.

This program includes: *The Creative Way in 5 Minutes a Day* workbook and program. https://masteringtheartoflife.com/creativeway/

Mastering the Art of Life Year-Long program

DESIGN – The first three months are The Creative Way. At first your vision will be like a sketched outline. As the program progresses and you go deeper, more details will reveal themselves to you. You'll learn how to use Universal Laws and practices to envision your dream life.

CRITIQUE the roadblocks in your way. All of us have unconscious limiting beliefs from the past that are keeping us stuck today. When you go deeply into this program you'll learn what those roadblocks and limiting beliefs have to teach you, and transform them into stepping stones toward your dream.

CREATE lasting results in living your life as a Masterpiece. Now that the roadblocks are supportive stepping stones; transform your goals and dreams into reality. You can begin to bring your Masterpiece into the world.

This program includes: 53 weekly recordings with workbooks, twice-monthly coaching. https://masteringtheartoflife.com/maol/